Practice makes perfect

# *Practice makes perfect*

## The book of James simply explained

### Anthony E. Bird

EP BOOKS
Faverdale North, Darlington, DL3 0PH, England

e-mail: sales@evangelicalpress.org

EP BOOKS INC.
P. O. Box 825, Webster, New York 14580, USA

e-mail: usa.sales@evangelicalpress.org

**web: http://www.epbooks.org**




First published 2009

**British Library Cataloguing in Publication Data available**

ISBN 13 978 085234 693 8          ISBN 0 85234 693 X




Printed and bound in the UK by the MPG Books Group

To my wife Carole,
companion and friend for over thirty years,
and to our family

# Contents

# Preface

The material in this book began to take shape from sermons preached for the people of Donvale Presbyterian Church in Melbourne, whose love and friendship have been a wonderful blessing from God during the past ten years. Some of the time needed to study and write on James was made available by the Theological Education Committee of the Presbyterian Church of Victoria through generous sabbatical leave arrangements. I want also to acknowledge the support and encouragement of the faculty of the Presbyterian Theological College, especially the principal, Dr Douglas Milne.

Although much attention has been given to the relationship between faith and works in chapter 2, James' comments on teachers (3:1) are more challenging and in my mind make it one of the most daunting of all New Testament books to write about. What follows is offered in the hope that it might stimulate prayerful study of the text of Scripture which alone is God-breathed.

I want to record my gratitude to Morag Zwartz, who read the manuscript in draft form and gave numerous valuable suggestions. Also my thanks go to Joan Milne for proofreading earlier versions, to David Clark, for his encouragement to write, and to Evangelical Press for the opportunity and privilege to contribute to this commentary series.

**Tony Bird**
Melbourne, 2009

# Introduction

Three things stand out when reading the letter of James. The first is the down-to-earth nature of the letter; the second is the diversity of the topics covered, making it hard to work out what the letter is about; and the third is the fact that the name of Jesus Christ is rarely mentioned. In this introduction, we will take up the three points in turn.

**James — a practical letter**

At first glance James appears to be one of the least doctrinal and most practical books in the New Testament. The letter is filled with advice about facing the trials of life, coping with poverty, the desire to be rich, controlling the tongue, making plans for the future, and so on. This makes it attractive to the pragmatic person, or to someone with a dislike for doctrine. James does underline the need to be active, practising believers. We are to be those who 'do not merely listen to the word' but 'do what it says' (1:22).

Nevertheless it is a mistake to read James merely as a handbook of helpful advice. We must not jump straight into the 'How?' without pausing to ask, 'Who?' Christianity is first and foremost about a relationship. Rightly relating to God through Jesus Christ is the beginning and end of the Christian life. If we treat this letter as a do-it-yourself manual of living, we run the risk of knowing a lot about Christian practice but little about God himself. In the end God will be as distant from us as when we began, and our practice may end up as a legalistic checklist of dos and don'ts. No matter how enthusiastically we embrace a practical approach to the Christian life, it has no value unless it is based upon God, who is the source of that life.

Closer inspection of the letter reveals the principle that, the better we know God, the better we become at living the Christian life. When James wants to make a practical application he appeals to some attribute or quality in God (1:5,17; 2:5,19; 3:9; 4:5-6,8,15; 5:11,15). So, for example, reminding ourselves of the generosity of God serves as an incentive to seek him prayerfully for wisdom in trials (1:5-8). Knowing that God is good will prevent us from attaching blame to him when temptations come (1:13-17). Recognizing God's impartiality will stop us from trying to play favourites (2:1-7). James is both doctrinal and practical in the sense that true knowledge of God informs and guides all practice in the Christian life.

What is remarkable about this letter is the glorious vision it presents of God, the descriptions of whom are both extensive and breathtaking. Reading it ought to drive us to contemplate afresh the wonder of God and then lead us to worship him. In fact the more we entertain true and great thoughts about him, the more we shall be in a position to face the trials of life, the attractions of the world, the ongoing battle with sin and the unrelenting hostility of the Evil One. In addition we shall also be better equipped to do what his word says — to be practical Christians who make a useful contribution to the church of Jesus Christ.

**James — what is he saying?**

As readers we are much more likely to find our way around a text if we can grasp the main idea(s) that an author wants to convey and follow the progression of thought. The letter of James proves difficult in this regard. It lacks flow and seems to consist of loosely connected ideas on a wide variety of topics. While the individual parts of the letter make sense, it is hard to grasp the purpose of the whole. Indeed, early assessments by scholars concluded that the epistle lacked any continuity and that there was no overall theme. It was regarded much as the treasury in a palace where a king might keep many of his most valuable possessions. In this analogy James was a treasure store where Christian readers could help themselves to precious traditions of spiritual wisdom according to their different needs.

It would be wrong, however, to conclude that the letter is without structure.

1. It has the form of a letter, beginning, as many ancient letters did, with the author's name, the intended recipients and greetings (1:1). It also continues as a letter in which the first readers are appealed to at frequent intervals as 'brothers' (1:2,16,19; 2:1,5,14; 3:1,10,12; 4:11; 5:7,9,10,12,19). A definite audience is in mind, one to whom the author is giving clear and compelling instruction.

2. There are sections that cohere together in terms of content (2:1-13 on favouritism; 2:14-26 on faith and works; 3:1-12 on the tongue).

3. The recurrence of themes such as the dangers associated with wealth and poverty (1:9-11; 2:1-7; 4:13-17; 5:1-6), the importance of prayer (1:5-8; 4:1-10; 5:13-18), patience in trial (1:2-4,12; 5:7-11), control of speech (1:13-15,26; 3:1-12; 4:11-12; 5:12), and practising the faith (1:22-25,27; 2:14-26; 5:19-20) provides threads of consistency through the letter.

4. James uses bridging words which end one section but are repeated in the next to form connections

(though these are occasionally lost in translation). The most striking example is found in the early part of chapter 1: 'greetings' (1:1) with 'joy' (1:2), 'trials' (1:2) with 'testing' (1:3), 'perseverance' (1:3) with 'perseverance' (1:4) and 'lacking' (1:4) with 'lacks' (1:5). Later in the same chapter, reference to the 'word' (1:18) is subsequently taken up and developed in terms of accepting the 'word' (1:21) and doing the 'word' (1:22).

5. The repetition of similar words or ideas creates a frame (called an *inclusio*) to help the reader see the beginning and end of sections (e.g. 'trials' in 1:2 and 1:12). These frames can further help in making sense of material found within them.

Even where there are no immediate linguistic clues to link sections together, it does not necessarily mean that the letter lacks coherence. The wider context nearly always proves beneficial for understanding relationships between diverse and apparently dissimilar topics. The unexpected introduction of wealth and poverty (1:9-11) in a section that deals with trials (1:2-12) suggests that these are connected in the author's mind. James may want his readers to understand both wealth and poverty as being types of trials, if not the crucial one that they were facing. Jesus, from whom James draws much of his inspiration, also warned of the power of wealth to steal away the loyalty of the heart from God (Matt. 6:24).

But, even so, we must not overemphasize these connections and feel it necessary to come up with a complex literary arrangement for James. The lack of detailed structure has not proved to be necessarily negative for its readers, and the letter does not need to follow the closely woven arguments found in some of Paul's letters. Many kinds of letters existed in the ancient world and were used for a variety of purposes.

This one from James might best be classified as an encyclical letter intended for general circulation (1:1). If so, he was writing for a wide audience and therefore we might expect him to touch upon a range of topics.

Having said that, is there one general theme under which we may subsume all the diverse topics that are dealt with? I think there is. Letters normally begin with matters of primary importance, and the opening section (1:2-18) does set out a general pattern for growth into Christian maturity. This template is subsequently applied to the situations facing the first readers (1:19 – 5:20).

James begins with a challenge to 'be perfect and complete, lacking in nothing' (1:4, RSV). Our understanding of 'perfect' must be drawn from the context. This is not perfection in the sense of sinlessness, for James recognizes the fact of ongoing sin in the believer (5:16). Rather the thought is of maturity, since a mature Christian is someone who is actively putting away sinful patterns of speech, attitudes and behaviour (1:21) and is seeking to practise a likeness to Christ in thought, word and deed. This is only possible for those who have been spiritually transformed by his grace through the word of truth (1:18). The general theme of the letter is about how, through trials, we may become mature by doing what the word says, while waiting patiently for the Lord's coming.

Happiness, not holiness, is sadly the quest of some. Such people want Jesus to forgive their sins, get them out of difficulties and bless them with a trouble-free existence. But they do not want him to interfere overmuch in their plans, or to insist on a radical change of lifestyle. To such this letter is disturbing. It is also confronting to all who are genuinely seeking to follow Christ, because the journey to maturity is not an easy one. Trials mark out the genuine road to godliness (1:2). If we are to navigate successfully through these trials we need wisdom (1:5), since the trials intended to bring us to maturity can also become temptations if we question the God who appoints them (1:13). Indeed, giving in to evil desires, or doubting God, leads us on another pathway that, if unchecked, ends in death (1:15). Yet trials have a glorious objective which will be realized at the Lord's coming (1:12). This hope sustains us in suffering, supplies the motive for the ethical imperatives and gives the encouragement we need to make the quest for maturity an urgent priority (5:7-11).

In the rest of the letter James moves from pattern to practice and from theory to application (1:19 – 5:20). The word of truth (1:18), instrumental in bringing spiritual life, must be not only heard, but obeyed. The emphasis on being a doer of the word (1:22,23,25) is strengthened by subsequent reference to 'the word' as law (1:25; 2:8,9,10,11,12; 4:11). A word spoken may be heard, but when it becomes a law it is to be obeyed.

The standard of our maturity is measured by the law of God (1:25; 2:8-12; 4:11-12). James applies the law to those who have already been transformed by grace (1:18). This is law in the new-covenant sense, as written by God on the heart of the believer and fulfilled by Christ, and obedience to which is empowered by the Spirit (see Jer. 31:31-34). Calvin says this application of the law to Christians is 'not a power to bind their consciences with a curse, but one to shake off their sluggishness, by repeatedly urging them, and to pinch them awake to their imperfection'. Christ has freed us from the curse of the law, but not from its commands. We know that the law is good because it reveals where we are immature and incomplete.

The law addresses three broad areas of our lives: our loyalty to God, our duty to our neighbour and our responsibility to ourselves. James takes up these areas of concern (1:19 – 5:20):

## *1. Our loyalty to God*

Our loyalty to God is primarily contested by the world which sets itself in opposition to his rule. The world in this sense is the surrounding, materialistic and godless culture of our age, with its false values, empty pleasures and vain ambitions (see 1 John 2:15-17). This is a fundamental concern to James because, when he deals with worldliness, he breaks off from his usual affectionate term of address, 'my brothers', and replaces it with the stinging and passionate rebuke, 'you adulterous people' (4:4).

## *2. Our duty to our neighbour*

Duty to our neighbour must be evident by more than mere words (2:16). 'Religion that God our Father accepts as pure and faultless' is practical, loving service, not sweet sentiment (1:27). The person who claims to be a Christian but ignores the needs of others is self-deceived (2:14). Indeed, the genuineness of faith is always confirmed by actions (2:22).

## *3. Our responsibility to ourselves*

Responsibility to ourselves finds its application in the area of self-control, where the chief (but not the only) application is to speech. James has much to say which challenges us with regard to control of the tongue and its ability to cause hurt and division in the Christian community (3:1-12).

Even though James also has in mind the individual, his letter is written to churches — communities of believers scattered among the nations (1:1). A distinctive literary feature of James is the way he addresses his readers as 'brothers' (note the plural).[1] By calling them brothers, he assumes not only a gracious work of Christ in the heart, but also a desire to be a doer of the will of God (Mark 3:35). This form of address also reveals the importance of good relationships in the church, as well as James' concern that they display in practice what they are called to be. The mature church is a community which practises loving service by actively caring for the needy (1:26-27), welcoming the stranger (2:1-13), guarding speech (3:2-12), avoiding worldliness (4:1-10) and praying for one another (5:12-18).

## James — a servant of Jesus Christ

Finally, students of the book of James have been puzzled by its lack of Christ-centredness. Martin Luther was critical on the grounds that, in his view, James does not show us Christ. A superficial reading of the letter might support Luther and suggest that Christ is not as prominent as in other parts of Scripture. It is true that there are few references to the name of Jesus, and there is no explicit mention of the cross or resurrection.

But was Luther correct? I think not. The hidden but firm foundation of all that James wrote is to be understood from his opening words describing himself as 'a servant of God and of the Lord Jesus Christ' (1:1). Let us look at how the Jesus whom he confessed as Lord and Christ appears in the letter.

### 1. In name directly and indirectly

The name 'Jesus' is found twice (1:1 ; 2:1). In both instances James joins two titles to the human name Jesus — namely, 'Christ' (which is the Greek equivalent to the Jewish title 'Messiah') and 'Lord', which ascribes deity and was used in this sense by the church from the earliest times (Acts 2:36).

The incarnation is presupposed when James joins the human name 'Jesus' to the divine name 'Lord'.

In addition, the name 'Jesus' is implied in other places. 'The noble name' (2:7) could be the name of God, but, given the context (2:1), it is more likely to be a reference to Jesus. Even if it relates to the name 'Christian' (as in 1 Peter 4:16), it is still an indirect reference to Christ. Besides the use of the title 'Lord' to refer to God (1:7; 3:9; 4:10; 5:4,10,11), other verses where the same title is used are almost certainly more specific, referring to Jesus as Lord. There are two instances where the title is linked to the *parousia*, or the return, of the Lord (5:7,8). The word *parousia* is nearly always associated in the New Testament with the expectation of Jesus' appearing at the end of history. 'The Lord's coming' is Jesus' coming (e.g. Matt. 24:37; 1 Cor. 15:23). Furthermore, there was a clear expectation in the preaching of the apostles that Jesus was the one appointed by God to be the Judge of mankind at the close of the age (Peter in Acts 10:42; Paul in Acts 17:31). Reference therefore to 'the Judge' (5:9) can only mean Jesus.

This exalted view of Jesus conforms to the way he is described in the rest of the New Testament.

## 2. In his teachings

Although there is less explicit mention of the name of Jesus than in other books of the New Testament, there is more of his teaching found here than in any other letter. One theologian claims that James contains more echoes of the teaching of Jesus than all of the other New Testament letters put together. In the 108 verses that make up the epistle, he estimates that there are an amazing seventy-four parallels with Jesus' teaching in the Gospels.[2] Others are generally more conservative in their estimates but agree with the observation.[3]

Below is a small selection of parallels between the teachings of James and Jesus, which come from the Sermon on the Mount. Whether James was present when that sermon was preached we do not know, but many of the parallels are drawn from that occasion.

| | | |
|---|---|---|
| James 1:2,12 | compare with | Matt. 5:10,12 |
| James 1:17 | compare with | Matt. 7:11 |
| James 1:20 | compare with | Matt. 5:22 |
| James 1:22 | compare with | Matt. 7:24 |
| James 2:5 | compare with | Matt. 5:3 |
| James 4:4 | compare with | Matt. 6:24 |

As well as such textual parallels, we should also compare topics Jesus taught which are discussed by James, such as inheriting the kingdom of God (James 2:5; Matt. 25:34), being perfect (James 1:4; Matt. 5:48) and becoming doers of the word (James 1:22-27, 2:14-26; Matt. 7:24-27; 25:31-46). In fact the coming of Jesus transforms James' presentation of Old Testament teachings and ideas. Law is not presented as Mosaic law, with an interest in the ceremonial and ritual. By linking 'the perfect law that gives freedom' (1:22-25) with 'the word planted in you' (1:21), James is thinking of the new-covenant promise made in the Old Testament that God would write his law on the hearts of his believing people (Jer. 31:31-34), which was fulfilled in Jesus.

The striking correlation between the letter of James and the teaching of Jesus, together with the scarcity of references to the person of Jesus, suggests that James can be thought of not so much as a letter *about* Jesus as one *from* Jesus.

We need to read James with a view to knowing God better, with a desire to grow in loving service, mindful that Jesus is Lord and allowing his teachings to shape our lives.

# 1.
# Who's who?

*Please read James 1:1*

In 2002 a controversial announcement was made concerning the discovery of a limestone box bearing the inscription, 'James, son of Joseph, brother of Jesus'. It belonged to an Israeli collector of antiquities who claimed that when he had bought it in Jerusalem some years previously he had not realized its true significance. Suddenly James became headline news across the world. Could it be that the name on the inscription was the same James mentioned in the New Testament as a brother of Jesus? (e.g. Mark 6:3). If so, the box would be the first known instance of Jesus' name being recorded in stone, and not just in documents of the period.

Archaeologists call the box an ossuary (from the Latin for 'bones') because it was used to hold the bones of a dead person after the flesh had naturally decayed. But the authenticity of the ossuary is in serious doubt because it was not found *in situ*,[1] because the names James, Joseph and Jesus were commonplace in first-century Palestine and might well belong to another James, and because the inscription had been cleaned at some point. Whether or not the artefact is genuine is not crucial for our study, but if it is, then the ossuary once contained the last remains of someone who could be the author of this letter.

**Who wrote this letter?** (1:1)

These days when someone makes a telephone call he usually introduces himself first, but with a letter we have to read to the end to find out who the writer is. New Testament letter writers reveal their identity straight away, much as in a modern phone conversation.

The name **'James'** is the New Testament equivalent of the Old Testament name Jacob. It was a common enough Jewish name in the first century, unlike Paul or Peter, whose names are unique in the New Testament. Several men named James are mentioned:

- James the son of Zebedee and brother of John (Mark 1:19)
- James the son of Alphaeus (Mark 3:18; Matt. 10:3)
- James the younger (Mark 15:40)
- James the father of Judas (not Iscariot, Luke 6:16)
- James the Lord's brother (Gal. 1:19, probably also the brother of Jude mentioned in Jude 1).

But which one of these wrote the letter? Or was the author another, unknown James? To help us decide we can learn a number of things about the author from his letter.

1. James gives few clues about his identity. He describes himself only as **'a servant of God and of the Lord Jesus Christ'** (1:1). He gives no personal information, as Paul does in his letters (e.g. Gal. 1:11 – 2:10), nor does he provide the names of any friends or associates about whom we do know something.

2. He tells us that he is *a 'teacher'* by his use of the word 'we' in 3:1. Unquestionably the content and style of his letter testify to his skill in communication. Today the office of teacher has been considerably

weakened and the role of those who teach sometimes reduced to classroom management techniques, or psychological ploys to coax unwilling students towards desired educational outcomes, but in the ancient world the teacher was highly respected and played an influential role in society.

3. He writes with *familiarity of the Bible*, mentioning some of the key names in Jewish history: Abraham, Isaac, Rahab, Job, Elijah and the prophets. He quotes from the Old Testament (2:8; cf. Lev. 19:18), or makes allusions to it (1:10-11; cf. Isa. 40:6-7). He also has a high regard for the law of God and frequently refers to it (1:25; 2:8,9,10,11,12; 4:11-12).

4. He *knows the land of Israel* — for example, the wild flowers dying in the scorching heat and winds of summer (1:10-11) — and its seasons: the phrase 'the autumn and spring rains' (5:7) especially applies to the climate of Palestine.

5. He writes with *marked authority*. One out of every five verbs used is a command, which is indicative of the position he held. Moreover, this seems to have been a circular letter addressed to scattered believers, not one with a limited, local readership. James is someone of stature whose leadership is widely esteemed.

6. He has a warm pastoral relationship with his readers, frequently calling them 'my brothers' (1:2; 2:1,14; 3:1; 5:19) and even 'my dear brothers' (1:16,19). Yet this is not blind friendship. He is not afraid to rebuke where necessary (2:4,20; 4:4,8,16), showing that the author has authority while not being authoritarian, and he prefers to describe himself as a 'servant'.

Of the potential authors of this letter only James the son of Zebedee and James the half-brother of Jesus would have had the status and authority to write a letter of this kind without finding it necessary to give additional information about themselves. It is unlikely that the son of Zebedee is the author because he was martyred at an early date in AD 44 (Acts 12:2), and in any case it is more probable that he would have identified himself as an apostle (as Peter and Paul do) rather than a servant. This leaves James the Lord's brother as the most likely author. Furthermore, this particular James gave a short speech at the Council of Jerusalem (Acts 15:13-21) which, in the opinion of some scholars, manifests similarities of vocabulary and style with this epistle.

But does the rest of the New Testament support the case for authorship of the letter by the Lord's brother? All four Gospels mention the family of Jesus, and two of them name James among his brothers and sisters (Matt. 12:46-50; 13:55-56; Mark 3:31-34; 6:3; Luke 8:19-21; John 2:12; 7:3-5). Presumably these were the children born to Mary and Joseph after the birth of Jesus. At first the family thought Jesus was mentally disturbed (Mark 3:20-21). They did not recognize his prophetic role (Mark 6:4), and would not believe his messianic claims (John 7:3-5). Then James became a disciple (when or how we do not know) and Jesus conferred upon him the distinction and privilege of a personal resurrection appearance (1 Cor. 15:7). Shortly afterwards we find him at prayer with the other disciples (Acts 1:14), a practice which is a key topic in his letter and one to which the early Church Fathers draw attention.[2]

Scripture does not record the transformation of James from disciple to church leader, but by the time of Peter's release from prison he had already risen to prominence (Acts 12:17). When the first council of the church — the Jerusalem Council — was convened, James was present and was not just a delegate. He presided over this important council, which was assembled to settle the status of Gentiles who had believed in Christ (Acts 15). His concluding speech displays the godly and practical wisdom that is also found throughout his letter (Acts 15:13-21). His interpretation of the Old Testament was decisive in settling the issue of the relationship between faith and works (see 2:14-26) and it is instructive for our interpretation of James chapter 2 that he was in agreement with the apostle Paul in this matter.

With Peter and John, he was by reputation one of the 'pillars' of the church (Gal. 2:9-10). The agreement worked out with Paul was that James, Peter and John would focus their ministry on the Jews. At the same time Paul was urged to remember the poor, and this practical concern for the poor is another crucial feature of James' letter (2:14-17). Later, when the apostles, Peter and John, had departed, he was left in charge of the Jerusalem church and exercised the kind of authority over circumcised believers that is replicated in his letter (Acts 21:18).

James had a close association with the apostle Peter, these two being the acknowledged leaders in the Jerusalem church (Gal. 2:9), and both were among the main speakers at the Council of Jerusalem (Acts 15). This close fellowship in the work of the gospel, plus a common heritage in background and culture, makes it likely that we should find some common material between their letters. For example, compare 1 Peter 1:6-7 with James 1:2-3, in their similar treatment of trials, and 1 Peter 5:5-11 with James 4:6-10, which both cite the identical quotation from Proverbs 3:34.

Nothing that we know about James from elsewhere in the New Testament weakens the case for his authorship. On the contrary, his familiarity with Jesus' teachings, his leadership of the Jewish church, his ministry to the circumcised, his practical application of Scripture to the issues of faith, his concern for the poor and his personal piety harmonize well with the contents and point to his authority.

Other than the Bible, what else do we know of James the Lord's brother? Sources outside the Scriptures take a great deal of interest in him. In fact for the first few centuries of the church James was better known outside the Bible than in it. Many historians are at a loss to explain this fact, but it is probably explained by the destruction of Jerusalem in AD 70 and the shift to a Gentile-dominated church.

Eusebius, an early church historian who lived in the fourth century, records some of the early traditions about James that are consistent with the piety of the writer of the letter. He tells us that James was nicknamed 'James the Just' because of his godliness and was held in great respect in the church and by the people of Jerusalem. Eusebius records that James spent so much time on his knees praying for the forgiveness of the people that his knees became as hard as those of a camel — which also fits the content of the letter. He was not just a hearer of the word but a doer, practising what he preached (1:5-8; 5:13-18).

The Jewish historian Josephus (like Eusebius) records the details of James' death. From this early record we can estimate that he died around AD 62. This date sets an upper limit on the dating of the letter. James deals with the re-lationship between faith and works (2:14-26) in a way which suggests that he had not read or heard Paul on the same subject, indicating that his letter predates the Council of Jerusalem (which was held about AD 49). If that is the case, then this letter is probably the earliest document in the New Testament.


**How does James introduce himself?** (1:1)

The highest authority that James claims for himself is that of **'a servant'**. In fact the literal translation is not 'servant' but 'slave'. There were many kinds of slaves in the Roman Empire, ranging from those who worked in the mines as a punishment for criminal activity, with no freedoms and low life expectancy, to those who were slaves in Caesar's household and held important positions of power and prestige. But James was culturally a Jew rather than a Roman and, seeing that he was steeped in the Scriptures, it is far more likely that he used the term 'servant' in the Old Testament sense. There we find it is used as a title denoting great honour. A servant was someone chosen by God to be a leader and to serve him and his people with humility and unswerving loyalty (Abraham, Gen. 26:24; Job, Job 1:8; Elijah, 1 Kings 18:36; the prophets, Jer. 7:25). God has called James to this privileged position.

This servant of God had an authority derived not from a natural, familial relationship to Jesus, nor from personal ambition, but from divine appointment. James writes with a humble authority that shows he understands his position primarily as a servant of the Lord irrespective of the advantages of being related to Jesus according to the flesh. It is with the authority of the Lord that James writes, and therefore we must be careful to hear his words with respect and obedience.

James also adds that he is **'a servant of the Lord Jesus Christ'**. What a wonderful expression of the change that the grace of God makes! He places Jesus, his elder brother, alongside God! This is the same Jesus with whom he grew up as a boy in Nazareth, who had shared with him the joys and sorrows of family life (possibly including the death of Joseph). Yes, at one time he rejected his older brother as the Christ (John 7:5), but now he can say, 'Jesus is Lord' (Rom. 10:9). If ever there was a clear affirmation of both the manhood and deity of Jesus it is this, from a man who knew him according to the flesh and also by faith as the Son of God incarnate.

## How does James describe his readers?

Having completed his introduction, James distinguishes his readers in two ways:

*1. By race*

They are part of **'the twelve tribes'**. This is an Old Testament designation for Israel based on the number of the sons of Jacob with their descendants (Gen. 49:28; Exod. 24:4). These tribes were redeemed by God out of slavery in Egypt and brought into the promised land as their inheritance. In the New Testament Jesus reconstituted Israel, choosing twelve disciples to be apostles (Mark 3:13-19). Later, Paul describes believing Jews and Gentiles together as the 'Israel of God' (Gal. 6:16) and, similarly, Peter, writing to a racially mixed church, calls them 'a royal priesthood, a holy nation' (1 Peter 2:9). The distinguishing mark of this new people of God is not physical but spiritual — i.e. faith in Christ (Gal. 5:6).

*2. By location*

The twelve tribes are **'scattered among the nations'** (literally 'in the dispersion'). In the Old Testament there was a dispersion of the Jews from the promised land, mainly by forced exile, first by the Assyrians and later by the Babylonians. This physical migration in Israel's history becomes a theological theme in the later prophets, who foresaw a day when God would graciously gather in his dispersed ones (Isa. 11:12; Zeph. 3:10). This promise of return from exile, though begun, was not really considered to have been fulfilled by New Testament times. In fact there were far more Jews living in the rest of the Roman Empire than in Palestine, as the crowds on the Day of Pentecost (Acts

2:9-11) and Paul's missionary journeys in Acts both confirm (e.g. Acts 13:13-43). Jews living outside Israel were referred to as belonging to the dispersion (John 7:35). So by New Testament times the word 'dispersion' carries both literal and spiritual connotations.

Both James and Peter address their readers as those residing in the dispersion (see 1 Peter 1:1), but they write as Jews from a Christian perspective. The Christian church, largely Jewish at first, also became scattered by persecution and suffered its own exile by dispersion to other lands (Acts 8:1-3). But it is unlikely that James would fail to look beyond the geographical to the spiritual condition of the people of God. Peter, with whom James was closely associated in gospel ministry, certainly does, writing of the exile from a spiritual and heavenly perspective (1 Peter 1:17). We, like those early readers, are living in exile from our true homeland (Heb. 11:13-16). Dispersed now in a hostile world, suffering for our faith, we shall nevertheless one day be gathered from all the surrounding nations (Mark 13:27; Luke 13:29). The address to the 'twelve tribes scattered among the nations' applies equally to the church today.

**What greeting does he send?** (1:1)

James sends a simple one-word salutation which is translated as **'Greetings'**. This is the same salutation as that found in the letter which James wrote to Gentile believers after the Council of Jerusalem (Acts 15:23). The word 'greetings' comes from the same family as the word 'joy'. May the same joy be ours as we study this letter.

Part I
Pattern for Christian maturity
(1:2-18)

# 2.
# Good grief



*Please read James 1:2-4*

*The trials that afflict you,*
*the sorrows you endure:*
*what are they but the testing*
*that makes your calling sure?*
(John Mason Neale 1818–1866).

*God whispers in our pleasures, speaks in our conscience,*
*but shouts in our pain. It is his megaphone to rouse a deaf*
*world* (Clive Staples Lewis, 1898–1963).

Sprinter Betty Cuthbert was given the nickname 'golden girl' by the Australian press in 1956. Altogether she won four gold medals in her Olympic career; then in 1969 she was diagnosed with multiple sclerosis and is now confined to a wheelchair. As a Christian, she spends as much time as she can telling others of the joy she has found in Jesus as her Saviour. She says, 'I have never once asked, "Why me?" Because I love God so much, I've always thought it must be for a reason.' Betty Cuthbert knows the truth stated in the opening verses of this letter.

James could have introduced the Christian life in so many ways, yet he chose to write about trials and how we are to face them. It may be surprising to consider trials as pure joy, but if we cherish a faith that is genuine and growth that is God-given, then we shall need to rethink our attitude to them. We are presented with a grander, more glorious vision of the Christian life than one that entails merely our own personal comfort and security.

Both Peter and Paul take a remarkably similar approach to James on this distinctive element of the Christian life (1 Peter 1:6-7; Rom. 5:2-5). All three look back to Jesus' teaching that we rejoice in suffering (Matt. 5:11-12).

**Finding joy in trials** (1:2)

Notice that James appeals first to the mind: **'Consider it ...'** (1:2). Right thinking always comes before right practice. For all his devastating criticism of a purely intellectual faith (e.g. 2:19), James is the first to appreciate the importance of right thinking for Christian maturity.

An oxymoron joins together two apparently contradictory ideas, as in the title of this chapter. Some are used as jokes, like 'government organization' or 'military intelligence', but others, like this one which links **'joy'** with **'trials'**, have the effect of grabbing our attention. This is not what we expect, or even what we want to hear. But considering trials as pure joy is in fact a crucial gospel issue. When things go wrong, the non-religious person may become stoic or bitter; a moralist may react with anger towards God ('I kept your standards and this is how you treat me') or self ('I have failed God and now he is punishing me'). But the believer trusts God in his trials because he knows he is the child of a loving heavenly Father.

Examples of wrong attitudes to trials abound in Scripture. The Exodus period provides a timely warning of the dangers of complaining at hardship (1 Cor. 10:10-13). Murmuring became the automatic response among the Israelites in the wilderness. On the other hand, Habakkuk's faith was tested by God's silence in response to his prayer about prevailing wickedness (Hab. 1:2-4). The Lord encouraged Habakkuk to live by faith in dependence on him and his word (Hab. 2:4) and Habakkuk responded with joy in his adversity (Hab. 3:17-18).

James is not saying that trials are good in themselves. The circumstances of trials must be distinguished from their purpose. Trials are distressing, and it would be unrealistic to say otherwise. Peter acknowledges this when he writes, 'You may have had to suffer grief in all kinds of trials' (1 Peter 1:6). But there is a joy that is independent of circumstances which may be found by remembering God's sovereignty and purposes.

The fact that we literally 'fall into' (not 'face' as in the NIV) these trials helps to narrow down what kind they are. The same word is used for the man who 'fell into' the hands of robbers in the parable of the Good Samaritan (Luke 10:30). This man did not create difficulties for himself; they were brought upon him. Similarly, the trials here are the afflictions that come upon us from outside. They are unlooked for and come unexpectedly. They are not the kind that we bring on ourselves by our own sinful choices or actions, although James does deal with these later, by counselling sorrow and repentance (4:1-10). Even those trials that are self-inflicted can be used by God for blessing.

The fact that they are **'trials of many kinds'** means that no one situation is in mind. The letter supplies clues as to what James may have had in mind. The specific trials affecting his readers include the poverty or wealth that threaten the integrity of faith (1:9-11), discrimination (2:1-4), oppression (2:6-7), slander (4:11-12) and serious illness (5:13-15). But we cannot reduce trials to these situations only. There may be tragedy, disappointments, unemployment, broken relationships, bereavement, or persecution — all of which are painful and bewildering. Yet we are to be ready, not if, but when they occur. They are part of God's will for us, and on the day of his coming (5:7) we shall thank him for every one of them.

By focusing on joy in trials James is not promoting some kind of higher life to be enjoyed only by a spiritual elite. Nor is he downplaying the joy that comes from the happy experiences of life, because all of God's gifts are good (1:17). Rather, his words are a reminder that faith is refined and grows strong in the soil of adversity — which is a realistic, unsentimental and much-needed view of the Christian life today.


**Tested faith produces endurance** (1:3)

God uses **'testing'** to strengthen faith, and James will refer later to the examples of some Old Testament figures who were tested (5:10-11). Yet the thought of testing faith conjures up the idea of a teacher setting an exam to test a student to see whether he will pass or fail. This is not what is meant. Rather, it is the idea of a precious metal that is heated in a crucible to refine it from impurities (Prov. 27:21). All the important things in life, such as the water we drink, the food we eat and the cars we drive, are tested for quality. But none is as precious as faith (1 Peter 1:7). God has a good purpose in testing us. It is to confirm, assure and strengthen (not to pass or fail) us in the school of faith.

The testing of our faith produces an intermediate virtue called **'perseverance'**. This quality is highly esteemed by the athlete who competes in a long-distance event like the marathon. Trials are divinely intended to produce stamina (as in Rom. 5:3), which is a necessary feature of the Christian's life (Matt. 10:22; 24:13; 1 Tim. 6:11; Rev. 2:10). Indeed, persevering in trials is necessary for sharing in future glory with Christ, as well as being the evidence of genuine faith now (2 Tim. 2:12).

## The goal of maturity (1:4)

We are much more likely to endure trials if we believe there is a good reason for them, because suffering which seems to serve no purpose is discouraging. The athlete puts up with discomfort in training to improve his future race performance. If there is no improvement as a result of all his training, he will soon give up. The side effects of chemotherapy are endured by patients because they believe that the drugs destroy cancerous cells and promote recovery. A woman in labour suffers at the same time as she looks forward with joy to the birth of a child. Christ endured with joy the humiliation of the cross because he looked beyond it (Heb. 12:2). Joy coexists with suffering where there are higher and better prospects in view. For us the great motivation to endure is to look to the end of the process in which God is at work.

Each of us has a duty to let perseverance **'finish its work'**. We have a responsibility not to close our hearts to the purposes of God in trials. There is a process which must be allowed to run its course if maturity is to be attained. Some versions of the Christian life teach the existence of distinctive blessings subsequent to conversion in order to fast-track spiritual maturity, but no such proposal is made by James. Fruit takes time to ripen before it can be harvested and enjoyed (5:7).

Perseverance is not an end in itself; it is only an intermediate stage to the goal of becoming **'mature and complete, not lacking anything'**. This goal could imply a faultless and impeccable life, but that cannot be the meaning since James says later that we all make many mistakes (3:2).

The concept is rather that of the development of a well-rounded Christian character, later explained in terms of a seamless life of hearing followed by doing (1:19-21), faith accompanied by works (2:14-26) and patience in the face of delay (5:7).

The word **'complete'** is used elsewhere in the New Testament of the wholeness of a healthy body in contrast to a sick one (Acts 3:16). James is encouraging a particular kind of maturity — an all-round maturity that is demonstrated by a likeness to Christ in every part of our character. **'Not lacking anything'** expresses negatively what 'complete' suggests positively. It is possible to grow only in selected areas of the Christian life, just as a child can advance in reading skills yet fall behind in social adjustment. God wants to see a complete formation of virtues in our lives.

John Newton, better known for his hymn 'Amazing Grace', also wrote the hymn below for publication in *Olney Hymns* in 1779. With moving clarity he conveys what we feel in the midst of trials as well as expressing God's purpose, which is to set us free from 'self and pride' and cause us to set our hopes on him alone.

> I asked the Lord, that I might grow
> In faith, and love, and every grace;
> Might more of his salvation know,
> And seek, more earnestly, his face.
>
> I hoped that in some favoured hour
> At once he'd answer my request,
> And by his love's constraining pow'r,
> Subdue my sins, and give me rest.
>
> Instead of this, he made me feel
> The hidden evils of my heart;

And let the angry pow'rs of hell
Assault my soul in every part.

Yea more, with his own hand he seemed
Intent to aggravate my woe;
Crossed all the fair designs I schemed,
Blasted my gourds, and laid me low.

'Lord, why is this?' I trembling cried,
'Wilt thou pursue thy worm to death?'
'' Tis in this way,' the Lord replied,
'I answer prayer for grace and faith.

'These inward trials I employ
From self and pride to set thee free;
And break thy schemes of earthly joy,
That thou may'st find thy all in me'
(John Newton, 1725–1827).

Maturity is not a goal that will ever be entirely achieved in this life, because we shall never be free of 'self and pride' until Christ comes and sin is no more. None the less this is God's purpose, and the hope of our glorious future provides us with the encouragement we need to progress towards it through trials.

# 3.
# Unconventional wisdom

*Please read James 1:5-8*

The plain truth of the matter is that we don't think very deeply about life while we are having fun. We are far too busy enjoying ourselves and having a good time to ask the deep and significant questions about who we are, why we are here and where we are going. Trials, however, have the tendency to cause us to reflect on what is really important.

> I walked a mile with Pleasure,
> She chattered all the way;
> But left me none the wiser,
> For all she had to say.
> I walked a mile with Sorrow,
> And ne'er a word said she;
> But, oh! the things I learned from her
> When Sorrow walked with me!
> (Robert Browning Hamilton, 1753–1809).

Of course it doesn't always follow that the person who goes through trials ends up wiser. There is nothing automatic about this process. Trials make some people angry with God and bitter at life. We can put on a brave face and think that by sticking it out we are pleasing God, but that is to mistake stoicism for faith. We need help in trials because we lack wisdom and cannot cope alone.

Verse 5 picks up on the idea of 'not lacking anything' from the previous verse and describes a lack of **'wisdom'**, which is something that we all suffer from because we have not yet reached perfection. Wisdom is the decisive factor that makes all the difference to the outcome of our trials. Accordingly, James counsels us to pray for wisdom, without which trials will not lead to maturity, but may even become the occasion of temptation (1:13).

We basically respond to trials in one of two opposite ways. The wise response is to count them all joy, learning from them and recognizing a deeper and gracious purpose leading us towards maturity (1:2-4). The foolish response is to become discouraged and doubtful of God's love (1:6-8).

In the Bible one person is associated with wisdom more than any other. King Solomon received this gift from the Lord through prayer (1 Kings 3:9) and, in addition to granting his petition, God also generously added other blessings. In 1 Kings 4:32 we are told that Solomon spoke 3,000 wise sayings, many of which are contained in the book of Proverbs and provide a sound footing for life and relationships. Wisdom is not just knowledge in general; it is the application of the Word of God to the problems and choices that confront us every day. This wisdom is not intellectual but spiritual, coming 'from heaven', from God himself (3:15,17).

We desperately need this virtue for all the key areas of our lives. It is necessary in marriage to avoid a build-up of bitterness and resentment. Parents need wisdom in teaching their children to resist the strong peer pressures to conform to the world. Church life would be enriched if we learned to love those with whom we might disagree. We require wisdom in order to live responsibly as citizens and not retreat from our duties and obligations in society. We need wisdom at every stage of life: when young, in choosing friends who will help us to grow in the faith; in the Gadarene rush of middle age to know how to set our priorities amidst competing pressures of family, church and work; in old age to trust God in increasing bodily weakness and to prepare ourselves for the great change when we are ushered into his eternal presence.


## Ask God for wisdom in trials (1:5)

In the pain of trials it is easy to rely on our own understanding or to look for well-meaning, feel-good advice, but if all we are looking for is pain relief we need paracetamol, not prayer. God's aim in trials is to make us holy, not happy. If that is not our aim we shall not find prayer helpful.

James not only indicates our need for wisdom: he goes on to tell us where to find it — **'he should ask God'**. In trials we must pray, not protest, because prayer is the practical expression of our dependence upon God, the visible exercise of our faith. It is not the least or the last thing we do; it is the first and the most powerful. We are later reminded that this action is so potent that Elijah could even invoke climate change through prayer (5:17-18).

Obtaining God's wisdom involves our participation. The Scriptures repeatedly invite us to desire and to seek it (e.g. Prov. 2:1-5). Wisdom comes from diligent and prayerful study of God's Word (Ps. 119:97-104). Notice the following encouragements.


*1. It is in the nature of God to give wisdom*

God is variously described in the Bible as holy, righteous, gracious, merciful and loving, but here as the one **'who gives'** (James literally describes him as 'the giving God'). Furthermore, God gives **'to all'**. There is a global commitment to his liberality. We may make distinctions in our generosity, but God's gifts go out to everyone (Matt. 5:45). When compared with our love, this is an uncomfortable reminder of the extent of God's generosity, which finds its ultimate expression in the giving of his one and only Son (Rom. 8:32).

## 2. God gives 'generously'

God does not promise to answer every prayer we make, any more than sensible parents comply with every request from their children. God loves us too much for that. Although **'generously'** suggests that God's giving is liberal — which he is — the original word has the root idea of someone who is uncomplicated.[1] Hence, in his giving, God has no ulterior motives. His giving is the pure, wholesome expression of his goodness. This may be the better way of understanding God's giving, especially as it is subsequently contrasted with our mixed and divided motives (1:7-8).

## 3. God gives graciously

As parents we may lose patience with our children when they make mistakes repeatedly, and we make sure they know they have messed things up long before we offer help. But God gives **'without finding fault'**; hence he does not confront us with a list of past failures when we come back to him again and again.

## 4. Possession of wisdom is promised

James gives an assurance that **'[Wisdom] will be given to him.'** The repetition in verse 5 of the verb 'to give', used first to describe God as 'the giving God' and then to indicate the outcome of prayer, joins together the cause of the promise with its effect. We can ask with confidence in prayer because it is in God's essential nature to give.

This is a promise reminiscent of Jesus' teaching on prayer, which also drives us back behind the petition to the goodness of the Father in heaven who delights to give good things to his children:

> Ask and it will be given to you; seek and you will find; knock and the door will be opened to you. For everyone who asks receives; he who seeks finds; and to him who knocks, the door will be opened.
>
> Which of you, if his son asks for bread, will give him a stone? Or if he asks for a fish, will give him a snake? If you, then, though you are evil, know how to give good gifts to your children, how much more will your Father in heaven give good gifts to those who ask him! (Matt. 7:7-11).

God pledges to supply our need so that we lack nothing for growth. God could no more refuse a believing prayer for wisdom than he could deny himself. Therefore we cannot justify our reluctance to pray out of fear of rejection or failure.

## Ask in faith, not doubting (1:6-8)

In a few words we are told of God's willingness to give, but James goes on to take much more space in telling us some realistic and unpalatable truths about ourselves. Why do we so often fail in trials? This is not because help is not to be had, nor because God does not want to grant us wisdom; rather it is because we doubt.

If it is in the very nature of God to give, where does our reluctance to **'believe and not doubt'** come from? Surely, it goes right back to the baneful effects of Adam and Eve's rebellion in the Garden of Eden. The serpent portrayed God as mean-spirited by focusing attention upon the fruit of the forbidden tree, deliberately overlooking the fact that God had given the fruit of *all* the other trees in the garden for food. Adam and Eve doubted God's generosity and if we follow their example we cannot expect him to hear our prayer.

But what kind of doubt is sinful? Many a Christian is troubled by doubts and has honest questions about the faith. Thomas doubted, yet his loyalty and love for Christ were never in question (John 20:24-25), nor was he was rebuked for his doubts (though his scepticism was not commended either). While some kinds of doubt indicate weak faith rather than no faith, there is a doubt that stems from unbelief. James likens the case of this person to **'a wave of the sea, blown and tossed by the wind'**, which is the first of many illustrations that he takes from the world of nature. Just as waves are at the mercy of the wind and its power, so doubters will become victims, rather than victors, in the trials of life.

The way some Christians pray is analogous to the nervous conversations of students waiting to go in to sit an exam. Someone will always insist that he hasn't done the study and has no hope of passing. It may make him feel better, but it is a psychological ploy. That person wants to cushion himself against the worst so that, no matter how poor his final results are, they will always be better than he feared. Some Christians pray in this way. It is possible for us to ask God hopefully, not really expecting anything from him, so we shall not be disappointed if we receive nothing (which is precisely what we get). James bluntly calls this being **'double-minded'**. Double-mindedness is faith in two minds: praying hopefully but expecting nothing.

The double-minded person is more often self-deceived than overtly hypocritical. On the one hand, he knows and approves what is good. He senses the generosity of God, the value of prayer and the need of wisdom, but in practice he is enslaved by his own passions. In the crisis of trials he puts self first.

The remedy for double-mindedness is simplicity, which is more than a lifestyle based on plain food or secondhand clothes and a small dwelling with modest furniture. The essence of simplicity is a mindset that has one loyalty and one agenda, which is Christ and his kingdom (Matt. 6:33).

Notice finally that the double-minded Christian will have problems in all areas of life. Poor praying is just one symptom of poor discipleship. The doubter shows an instability **'in all he does'**. It is worth noting that the word translated **'unstable'** occurs only here and in James 3:8, where it is used to label the tongue as 'restless'. The word indicates someone who is always changing, ever inconsistent — a malaise that affects not only a person's praying, but the whole of his life. What is required is repentance and the renewal of an unreserved trust in God.

# 4.
# How we are to think of ourselves



How do you like to think of yourself? What kind of self-image do you have? Some people define themselves by their physical appearance, others by their athletic prowess, still others by their intellectual capacity. Arguably though, wealth (or poverty) has the greatest potential to establish an identity for us. Our economic situation is still probably the most socially defining factor in our relationship with others and our attitude to ourselves. Notice how people's behaviour changes depending on whether the person they are dealing with is either rich or poor (2:1-4).

Wealth and poverty are always relative. What a Western government defines as poverty would be regarded by comparison as wealth in a Third World country. In the first century, when James was writing, poverty would have meant minimal levels of food, clothing and shelter, together with little or no access to medical services or education. But James is not trying to define poverty and wealth. By placing them alongside each other he has in mind believers who are in the same congregation and he is writing about them in a comparative way. What he says has enduring application since in almost every congregation there is a socio-economic mix.

James does not try to eliminate economic differences by encouraging the wealthy to give to the poor. That is not his purpose here, though the pressing need to help the poor could be inferred from elsewhere in his letter (2:15-16). He does not shame the poor brother by highlighting his poverty; nor does he condemn the rich brother for his wealth. But he points to something they both have in common, which is their faith in Jesus. This has brought them together and is now the most important factor in their relationship. They are brothers (and sisters) because of what God has done for them in Christ. This is the great leveller that makes all other distinctions (including wealth) pale by comparison.

From the context (see the introduction), James regards wealth or poverty as one of the great trials his readers were experiencing. There is nothing quite like abundance, or lack, to expose where the true loyalties of the heart lie. There are few tests of faith quite as rigorous. Pride (Ezek. 28:5), envy (Prov. 24:19), self-sufficiency (Prov. 28:11), worry (Eccles. 5:12), sensual indulgence (5:5), theft (Matt. 6:19), violence (5:6), oppression (5:4), and much more, are all traced back to money, or the lack of it. James urges us to pray when we fall into trials (1:5-8) and the book of Proverbs suggests a prayer we might use when our faith is tested by material abundance or scarcity:

> Give me neither poverty nor riches —
> Feed me with the food allotted to me;
> Lest I be full and deny you,
> And say, 'Who is the LORD?'
> Or lest I be poor and steal,
> And profane the name of my God
>
> (Prov. 30:8-9, NKJV).

What is not immediately obvious is whether James is addressing wealthy believers or wealthy unbelievers. He does not explicitly refer to the rich person as a 'brother'. He describes him in less than promising terms: the rich man **'will pass away like a wild flower'** (1:10) and **'will fade away even while he goes about his business'** (1:11). The rest of the letter might also suggest that the rich are ruthless and oppressive (2:6; 5:1-6). However, the evidence is not conclusive, because the rich man is directly addressed as if he was a member of the 'twelve tribes scattered among the nations' (1:1). Moreover, the natural parallelism with verse 9 suggests that he is a **'brother'** in Christ. We also know from the rest of the letter that there were wealthy men among the churches to whom this teaching would apply (4:13). It does seem, then, as though James is writing to churches consisting mainly of poor people, but with a minority who were well off — a social mix that would have the potential to create tensions in the fellowship.

The basic principle is that we should learn to think of ourselves not according to our economic circumstances, but by what we have become in Christ. King Edward VIII is the only British monarch to have voluntarily abdicated the throne, doing so to marry Mrs Wallis Simpson, an American divorcee. In a radio broadcast he once described his relationship with his father, King George V. When, as a child, he had done something wrong his father, who was a strict disciplinarian, would say in a stern voice, 'Young boy, you must always remember who you are!' In other words, if he had kept in mind that he was a member of a royal household and would one day inherit the throne he would have behaved differently. In a similar way, James is implying that the Christian life properly lived depends on knowing and remembering who we are. Our true identity is now defined by our relationship to Jesus Christ and not by possessions (or anything else). The poor believer and the wealthy one are to think of themselves differently: they are both to **'take pride in'** the new position created by faith in Jesus Christ. James presents us in embryonic form with a paradigm for Christian growth (sanctification) which Paul later develops in terms of our faith-union with Christ (Rom. 6 – 8).


**Poor but rich** (1:9)

The **'brother in humble circumstances'** (1:9) is directly contrasted with **'the one who is rich'** (1:10). He is the brother who is struggling to live on meagre resources — someone with no economic power and consequently little social standing. But that person is still a **'brother'** — as, for example, Lazarus, whose only home in this world was a pitch outside a rich man's gate (Luke 16:20-22). He (or she) is a person for whom Christ died.

It is easy for us to construct our identity on the basis of the outward trappings of prosperity, such as fashionable clothes, a late-model car and a spacious house furnished with luxury goods. We readily confuse wealth with worth, riches with rank. But it is possible to be a millionaire yet impoverished, or a pauper yet rich. The temptation for the poorly-off brother is to feel shame and self-pity because of his situation in life; however, from the perspective of faith the reality is quite different. The poor believer is told to **'take pride in his high position'**. What really matters is the elevated status that faith in Christ confers. He, or she, is a child of the King, a member of a royal household who will one day inherit the kingdom that God has promised to those who love him. Even now he has been endowed with a richness of faith that is of far more value than precious metals such as gold or silver (1 Peter 1:7; see also James 2:5).

## **Rich but poor** (1:10-11)

The Bible regards wealth properly acquired as a blessing from God. Yet the dangers it introduces into our relationship with God are such that biblical teaching on it is largely cautionary. The first mention of wealth in the Bible occurs in Genesis 13:2. The wealth that Abraham had acquired in Egypt from Pharaoh later became the source of a family feud (Gen. 13:5-7). Moses warned that wealth would bring the temptation to forget God (Deut. 8:13-14). Jesus warned his disciples that life does not consist in the abundance of things (Luke 12:15). In the Sermon on the Mount Jesus taught that material concerns can easily crowd out spiritual matters (Matt. 6:25-33). Some of our Lord's most memorable parables involve the dangers of wealth (Mark 4:19; Luke 16:19-31). The admonition that it will be hard for those who have riches to enter the kingdom of God still stands (Mark 10:23).

The rich believer is tempted to think too highly of himself because of the status that wealth brings. Mark Twain once wrote, 'The offspring of riches [is] pride, vanity, ostentation, arrogance, tyranny.' Wealth can easily generate pride because a rich man is treated differently; people flatter, or at least respect him and defer to his opinion. Before long he begins to believe the flattery. By contrast, James advises that he **'should take pride in his low position'**. He is not to think of himself in terms of his material success, nor become distracted by wealth and the lovely things it will buy. He is instead to remember the lesson of the wild flower.

One of the features of the land of Palestine is that the whole countryside is quickly covered with wild flowers after rain. But the colour and beauty are short-lived. The summer heat and scorching wind quickly return the landscape to a barren desert. This same picture is used by the writers of the Old Testament and applied to the transitory nature of life (Ps.

103:15-16; Isa. 40:6-8). James draws upon this natural phenomenon to explain how the ephemeral glory of wealth and the brevity of life should serve as a sobering reality check for all who are rich (cf. 1 Tim. 6:7). Riches confer no status in God's kingdom; neither do they count in the face of death, judgement and eternity. Rather, the wealthy believer is to rejoice in his low position by humbling himself before God and take pride in his relationship with Christ, who was gentle and lowly in heart and who was despised and rejected by the world. Those of us who are rich need to spend far more time thinking about what the gospel has done for us and about Christ's eternal kingdom which is coming.

Notice that the rich man is described as a man who **'goes about his business'** — i.e. the activity and opportunities that wealth affords and the world admires. But a full social life and absorbing interests create the illusion that the lifestyle wealth affords goes on for ever. In one of the parables of Jesus a rich man hosts daily dinner parties with lavish entertainment which diverts him from the far more pressing matters of the state of his own soul, evidenced by his neglect of the beggar Lazarus at his gate (Luke 16:19-31).


**Look to the future** (1:12)


Verse 12 returns to the topic of trials introduced at the beginning of the letter (1:2-4) and closes off this section. Blessing is promised to all who persevere under trial (1:12). Some English versions of the Bible translate verse 12 as, 'Happy is the man...', which might suggest an emotional high, but it is highly unlikely that we shall feel bright and cheerful in the midst of trials. Historically the word 'happy' also means 'blessed', or 'divinely favoured', which is what is intended here. **'Blessed is the man...'** speaks of God's disposition towards us rather than our mental or emotional state.

If our goal in life is to become as wealthy and comfortable as we can for our 'threescore years and ten', then the promise of a crown of life will hold little attraction. But if we understand that our future is bound up with the service and worship of God in eternity, and if we want to live now in such a way as to hear the words, 'Well done, good and faithful servant!' (Matt. 25:23), then the crown of life will be precious to us. We need to ask, in the context of a society in which for many the only goal in life is to work hard for a comfortable retirement, what are our ambitions? How do our goals affect the way we face trials? Are we those whose values and conduct are shaped by eternity?

Great reward is promised to those who endure trials. This is a certain promise (**'he will receive'**) and also a glorious one (**'the crown of life'**). A crown symbolizes both status and reward. A person who wore a crown was someone of rank and dignity (Rev. 4:4,10). This future position of high honour bestowed by God is in contrast to present lowliness. A crown also signifies reward. An athlete might achieve a fading wreath in the arena if victorious (1 Cor. 9:25), but the reward promised here is everlasting life, which is nothing less than life with Christ. This crown is promised to **'those who love him'**. The crown of life is not given to a spiritual elite, but to everyone who truly loves God.

# 5.
# Have we trials and temptations?

*Please read James 1:13-15*

Why James changes topic from *trial* (1:12) to *temptation* (1:13) is not as obvious to us as it would have been to the first readers of his letter. The two different words in English translate expressions which come from the same root in the original language. The choice whether to translate one way or the other is always determined by the context. But there is, I suspect, another reason why these two are linked. Although we may be able to make a distinction in theory between trial and temptation, this is not so easy in practice. Every trial has the potential to become temptation when not met with faith, because it strikes an answering chord in our hearts from what James calls **'evil desire'** (1:14). Trials may lead us, for example, to wallow in doubt instead of seeking the Lord in prayer (1:5-6). Poverty may result in envy instead of our taking pride in our high position (1:9).

While we were living in Scotland some years ago, a leader of our local church, together with his wife, sought to give practical help to a lonely woman whose marriage had broken down. To give her a rest they took her on a holiday. During the holiday the church leader's wife found that she became the odd one out, and eventually her own marriage ended. The presence of a third party in the family was both a test and a temptation. As a test it should have led to the husband's cleaving to his wife, to a stronger marriage and a genuine ministry to someone in need. As a temptation it led the man to commit adultery.

What James presents can be thought of as a basic paradigm of growth or decay. Trials may lead either into a cycle of growth towards Christian maturity, or into one of decay leading to spiritual death. In one cycle, 'trials of many kinds' lead to 'the testing of your faith', which in turn 'develops perseverance'. The finishing of perseverance produces the desired outcome of being 'mature and complete, not lacking anything' (1:2-4). Conversely those very same trials may inflame 'evil desire' within, which, once conceived, 'gives birth to sin', and that sin, 'when it is full-grown, gives birth to death' (1:13-15). It is this latter cycle that is the focus of our interest in this chapter.

## Blame shifting (1:13)

With temptation comes the tendency to doubt God's good will towards us by saying, **'God is tempting me.'** Thus not only do the evil desires of our heart lead us to sin, but in addition we try to excuse our stupidity by blaming God when sinful choices ruin our life. 'A man's own folly ruins his life, yet his heart rages against the LORD' (Prov. 19:3).

Blaming God is the oldest known response to temptation. After Adam had succumbed to temptation and had eaten of the forbidden fruit from the tree of the knowledge of good and evil, he said to the Lord God, 'The woman you put here with me — she gave me some fruit from the tree, and I ate it' (Gen. 3:12). Not only is it the woman's fault, but God is also made responsible: 'You put her here with me'! Thus sin becomes compounded by contempt for the Lord.

James traces blame-shifting back to distorted ideas of God, according to which he might somehow want to lead us astray. Once again this very practical letter makes it clear that, the better we know the true God, and not some caricature, the better we shall live for him. Our practice is only as good as our theology.

God knows of evil. But, more than that, he ordained evil and planned in eternity to send his one and only Son to deal with it and to one day come again to remove every evil thing from his world. Indeed, we can say that from all eternity God freely and wisely ordained everything that takes place (Eph. 1:11), but in such a way that he is neither the author of evil, nor is he affected by it, nor does he violate the will of his creatures to induce them to commit evil (1 John 1:5). Because God is pure goodness, there is nothing in him to which evil could ever appeal. The character of God is such that he **'cannot be tempted by evil, nor does he tempt anyone'**. It is therefore inconceivable that he would desire evil to be brought out in us. This is the counter-argument that James presents when we foolishly try to blame God for temptations.

But someone will ask, 'Why, then, does the Bible speak of God being tempted?' (Exod. 17:7; Deut. 6:16; Acts 15:10). Modern translations such as the NIV render these occurrences using the word 'test' (hence, 'Do not test the LORD your God...' Deut. 6:16), not 'tempt', as in older versions like the KJV. The point is different from the one which James is making — namely, that we have no right to challenge God to prove his power, presence or character unless specifically invited (e.g. Mal. 3:10). To do so shows unbelief and a failure to take God at his word.

What, then, is God's involvement with the temptations which lead us to evil and the trials which test our faith? We could say that God stands behind both, though in different ways. He stands behind our temptation not as its cause, but as the one who nevertheless has absolute control over it. He can use the evil done by us or to us for his glory, for nothing stands outside the sphere of his sovereignty (Eph. 1:11). By contrast, he stands behind trials in such a way as to use them for our growth in grace (1:2-4). He never uses trials to destroy our faith, but to strengthen it. This means that we can trust him in the bad times and praise him for the good ones.

In the midst of temptation our natural tendency is to blame anything or anyone, rather than accept responsibility ourselves. We cast blame upon our environment, our genes, the bad example of our parents, our socio-economic position and God, saying, 'God has made me this way; who am I to resist a sovereign God?' We even say, 'The devil made me do it.' We may try to minimize our responsibility, but making excuses and finding fault are indicative of personal guilt and a failure of faith.

## The mechanism of temptation (1:14)

> Thou knowest that thou hast formed me
> with passions wild and strong.
> And listening to their witching voice
> has often led me wrong.

The lines quoted above were written by Robert Burns, the Scottish poet. He had reason to pen the reference to his passions leading him astray, having just fathered an illegitimate child, but he had no cause to blame God for his own actions, for temptation works by appealing to *our own* evil desires (1:14). It is an axiom of Scripture that we are accountable for our actions. Although the devil may have been involved and we can never escape the sphere of God's sovereignty, the Bible is never more clear than it is in asserting that *my* sin is always *my* responsibility.

Temptations are always appealing; otherwise they would have no power over us. The language James uses to describe the mechanism of temptation comes from the world of fishing. **'Dragged away'** suggests the picture of a fish that has been hooked. To be **'enticed'** suggests being attracted by bait or a lure. The beautiful mayfly only lives for a day and hovers above the waters of rivers and lakes. Its feathery imitation tied onto a hook by a fly fisherman on a warm summer evening proves irresistible to trout or salmon. It takes skill to catch a fish in this way, but caught they often are, and so are we. Sinful responses always bring a pleasurable experience, or gratification of a desire, or some advantage or convenience. Temptation can come in many forms. Though evil desires within us may at times seem dormant, they quickly rise to the surface again, given the right combination of circumstances. They appeal powerfully to the weaknesses in each one of us, leading us to ask, 'Why not?' or 'Everyone else does it; why shouldn't I?'

**The progress of temptation** (1:15)

The progress of temptation is now described using the illustration of a life cycle. As soon as we say 'yes' to a temptation, we set in motion a chain of events as certain and as natural as childbirth itself. Once the egg in the womb has been fertilized, developments take place which lead nine months later to a new life being born. The fruit of evil desire, however, is a most unwelcome development. This child's name is **'sin'**, and when it grows up it **'gives birth to death'**.

The power of temptation lies in its appeal to an enemy called **'desire'** within the gates of the citadel of the heart. Therefore, no matter how strong the fortress, the presence of a traitor inside, ready to open up to the enemy, is a constant threat. It may be pride, as in the case of Hezekiah (2 Chr.

32:25), or covetousness, as with Achan (Josh. 7). For Peter it was fear (Matt. 26:69-75). Demas fell in love with this world and deserted the apostle Paul (2 Tim. 4:10). Diotrephes was a church leader consumed by ambition (3 John 9). We may never know the potency of our **'evil desire'** until temptation stimulates and inflames it.

What will keep us from being **'dragged away and enticed'**? Will fear of losing our reputation in the church? Will the thought of the resulting shame be an adequate defence? Or will the loss of peace of conscience, or even the fear of hell itself, keep us from giving in? None of these things is to be relied upon, though they may prevent gross acts of sin. When we say we can resist and don't need help, we show that we have not grasped where our true hope lies. Confidence in any of our natural strategies or strengths is a sure sign of weakness. If we enquire, 'What is our weakness?', the answer is that we are weakness itself.

When temptation strikes, our first recourse should be to the knowledge that, apart from the grace of God, we shall fail. Paul says, 'Let him who thinks he stands take heed lest he fall' (1 Cor. 10:12, NKJV). Peter, who loved the Lord so much and who failed so publicly, reminds us that we are kept by the power of God (1 Peter 1:5). The Puritan John Owen advises us when tempted to 'let the heart commune with itself and say, "I am poor and weak."'

We should pray, as John Owen exhorts: 'He that would be little in temptation, let him be much in prayer.' James has already mentioned the role of prayer in trials (1:5). We need wisdom from the Lord to strengthen and keep us from yielding to the evil desires within each one of us.

Finally, we must lay hold of the promises of Scripture. God is faithful, and with every temptation he will provide a way of escape so that we may be able to bear it (1 Cor. 10:13). There is the help of Christ (Heb. 2:18; 4:15-16), who can deliver us from the Evil One (Matt. 6:13). We are to put on the whole armour of God (Eph. 6:13). When we find special difficulties we should share our burden with others and if necessary make ourselves part of an accountability group.

Yield not to temptation, for yielding is sin;
Each victory will help you some other to win;
Fight manfully onward, dark passions subdue;
Look ever to Jesus, he will carry you through.

*Ask the Saviour to help you,*
*Comfort, strengthen and keep you;*
*He is willing to aid you,*
*He will carry you through*
(Horatio Richmond Palmer, 1834–1907).

# 6.
# God is good



*Please read James 1:16-18*

*How good is the God we adore,*
*Our faithful, unchangeable Friend!*
*His love is as great as his power,*
*And knows neither measure nor end!*
(Joseph Hart, 1712–1768).

Harry and Ruth were missionaries in the Yunan province of China. They had been bombed by the Japanese, shot at by the Communists and then forced to leave the country by the new government in 1950. Harry subsequently went into parish ministry in Australia. Later one of their sons, a pilot with a missionary organization, was killed in a plane crash. When I knew them in retirement Ruth's bones were so brittle that the slightest knock would cause bruising and possible fractures. Harry's health was little better. Yet in all the time I knew them I did not detect a trace of self-pity or complaining towards God — in fact just the opposite. There was a sweetness of character and a quiet confidence in God's goodness in their lives. How does one become like that? How does one avoid becoming bitter at the trials of life?

James has already offered several principles to follow when we face trials. We are to recognize their purpose

(1:2-4), to seek God's wisdom (1:5) and to remember who we are (1:9-11). We look to the future (1:12) and in no way do we blame God for our difficulties (1:13). James concludes this opening section by suggesting one final principle, which is to remind ourselves of God's goodness (1:16-18).

This short passage consists of a lovely description of the goodness of God. It is a necessary and welcome one in the light of the previous verses on temptation. We have discovered that God has no part in temptation to sin, nor can he be tempted by evil. But James is not content to leave the matter there. He wants to do more than refute the charge that God tempts us. He goes further by positively affirming that God and all his gifts are good. In the previous section he was defending the character of God; now he is promoting it.

This approach is instructive. First, it tells of the need to be sensitive to the honour of God — not only to defend, but also to promote his reputation, which is an application of the Third Commandment (Exod. 20:7). The positive attitude which this commandment encourages is to take the Lord's name seriously. Similarly, Jesus taught his disciples to hallow the Father's name (Matt. 6:9). His name is hallowed when we give him the honour he deserves in how we think about him, speak of him and live for him.

Notice too the balance. Until now much of the letter has been taken up with trials and temptations, so that we could easily go away with the impression that being a Christian is all about hardships and difficulties. Older members of a church can easily blunt the zeal of a young believer by warning of the many setbacks and disappointments in store for each of us. Even though this may at times be true, we should not give the impression that the Christian life is entirely negative. James shows balance, and so must we. God's rich blessings permeate our lives and we should be thankful in response.

## Don't be deceived (1:16)

Deception is an important theme in James. We can be deceived by a variety of sources. The devil disguises himself as an angel of light (2 Cor. 11:14) and deceives us into thinking that sin carries no consequences. We can also be deceived by others (Matt. 24:24), but deception in James' letter is invariably self-deception (1:16,22,26). For this reason James gives an affectionate warning (addressing his readers as **'my dear brothers'**) not to mislead ourselves about the nature of God in trials. In painful circumstances we can easily question the goodness of God and entertain unworthy thoughts about him.

## One who is unchangeably good (1:17)

In the introduction we saw that true knowledge of God is intimately related to the practice of the Christian life. If we entertain hazy notions about God, then the exercise of our faith will be confused. The doctrines of God are not take-it-or-leave-it matters best relegated to abstract theological debate by scholars. All the failures we experience in living out our faith can ultimately be traced back to defective ideas of God. So James points us to the unchangeable character of the God above, who gives **'every good and perfect gift'**.

Out of all the rich and glorious attributes of God, James selects his goodness for special attention. A well-known hymn is based on the ideas expressed in this verse:

Great is thy faithfulness, O God my Father!
There is no shadow of turning with thee;
Thou changest not, thy compassions, they fail not:
As thou hast been thou for ever wilt be
(Thomas O. Chisholm, 1866–1960).

Goodness is the one quality James singles out over which we can be deceived when trials come, but the God we are tempted to blame for our troubles is good, and his goodness is described in two ways.

### 1. *God's goodness is far-reaching*

The NIV text abbreviates the original Greek, which literally reads as 'every good giving and every perfect gift'. James emphasizes, by repetition of the word **'every'**, the all-encompassing quality of God's generosity. The psalmist similarly calls us to remember the wide-ranging nature of his goodness: 'The LORD is good *to all*; he has compassion on all he has made' (Ps. 145:9, italics added). The psalmist then lists his good gifts: he upholds us when we fall (v. 14); he provides our daily food (v. 15); every innocent pleasure (v. 16) and each gracious deliverance (v. 20) are traced back to God. In like manner throughout this letter the wonderful variety and richness of God's generosity are on display. He gives wisdom (1:5; 3:17), the crown of life (1:12), richness of faith (2:5), a kingdom (2:5), mercy (2:13), righteousness (2:23), grace (4:6), healing from sickness (5:14-16), rain (5:18) and salvation (5:20).

### 2. *God's goodness is constant*

God is described as the **'Father of the heavenly lights'** — the only occurrence in Scripture of this title for God. It is a reference to the sun, the moon and the stars (Gen. 1:14-16). James, ever the naturalist (see for example 1:6-8,10-11), observes the variation of these lights. They are in constant motion in the sky, always changing their positions and given to mark the times and seasons. The movement of these heavenly lights casts earthly shadows that are forever shifting. The illustration contrasts the created order and the

Creator — shadows shift; God is fixed. The universe is constantly changing, but God does not. What an encouragement in our rapidly changing world! Governments change; technology changes; people change; values and morals change. Yet in the midst of so much change the believer can say there is a fixed moral centre to this universe, an absolute in a relativistic culture.

George Müller of Bristol was a man of great faith who built orphanages and cared for the needy in nineteenth-century England. When his wife died of rheumatic fever in 1870, he preached a funeral sermon on the text: 'You are good, and what you do is good; teach me your decrees' (Ps. 119:68). The three points of his sermon were:

- The Lord was good, and did good, in giving her to me.
- The Lord was good, and did good, in so long leaving her to me.
- The Lord was good, and did good, in taking her from me.

George Müller was convinced that when things go wrong in our lives, and when our faith is put to the test, God has not changed his attitude towards us. He is the same yesterday, today and for ever.


**His goodness demonstrated in the new birth** (1:18)

How do we know that God is good? How else but in his choosing **'to give us birth'** — the new birth, which is the best and most gracious expression of his goodness? If we are believers, then our first and last thought each day should be of his goodness to us expressed in the salvation he made possible by the sacrifice of his one and only Son.

God chose to give us life **'through the word of truth'** — that is, the gospel message. Spiritual life comes through the instrument of the Word of God, which is to be believed because it is **'truth'** — the truth about God, about the world, about ourselves and about our sin and our need of Christ. If we wish to experience this new birth we must read the Bible and believe its message. When we do so, we experience the transforming power of God in our lives. If we do not, we die in our sin.

Eta Linnemann was the first woman to hold a professorship of New Testament in a German University. She was a disciple of Rudolph Bultmann, who persuaded a generation of students that there was little of historical value in the Gospel accounts about Jesus. As such she was a product of an unbelieving scholarship that has been highly influential for the last fifty years in theological circles. But she was plagued with personal problems — alcoholism and a growing disillusionment with her work. Then she came into contact with vital Christianity and God turned her life around. She left her university position, repudiated her writings in theology and became a missionary in East Java. Her latest books were written to defend the authority of Scripture and promote the truth that she had found. In one of them she writes:

My destructive addictions were replaced by a hunger and thirst for his Word and for fellowship with Christians. I was able to recognize sin clearly as sin rather than merely make excuses for it as was my previous habit. I can still remember the delicious joy I felt when for the first time black was once more black and white was once more white; the two ceased to pool together as indistinguishable grey.[1]

That is the new birth — the transforming power of God, brought about by the word of truth and in turn creating a love for that truth.

God's purpose in the new birth is **'that we might be a kind of first fruits of all he created'**. The phrase **'first fruits'** has an Old Testament background. When the harvest came, the first sheaves cut were offered to the Lord who had blessed his people with a fruitful crop. But those first fruits also spoke of the full harvest yet to be gathered in. James applies this figure to the Christian. We are the first sign that God will fulfil all his promises and make a new heaven and a new earth. We are the first ripe fruits of a cosmic event in which God will make all things new.

I once walked through the night in the high Alps in Victoria, Australia. At first light the quiet of the night gave way to a general stirring throughout the forest. The birds began to sing, the tops of the hills became tinged with orange and the sky to the east turned from black to blue. These were the first heralds of a new day. Likewise the existence of God's people is the first sign of a new and glorious age. The spiritual harvest begun is a sure sign of the triumph of the crucified Son. It is a sign and seal of the victory of the Holy Spirit. We are the children of God, the children of the resurrection age. We belong to the future and have crossed the great divide from death to life. We are the beginnings of what God will recreate and make good and holy. Praise his name!

Part II
Practice of Christian maturity
(1:19 – 5:20)

# 7.
# The good life

*Please read James 1:19-21*

The durian is prized in south-east Asia as the queen of fruits. From Myanmar to Irian Jaya, eating durian distinguishes you not just as a person of good taste, but as one who is appreciative of local culture. Unfortunately a ripe durian smells like a leaking septic tank! One tourist guide described the flesh inside as onion-flavoured custard squeezed through a sweaty sock! It is an acquired taste and also an expensive one. At harvest time the Javanese villagers where we used to live would place a guard around the trees to prevent theft.

On one occasion I decided to purchase three of the durian fruit from a local seller at the side of the road. Having a white face and a foreign accent is a distinct disadvantage in the slow but necessary art of bargaining. The price immediately goes up because all Westerners are considered wealthy. During the negotiations the seller cut a wedge out of one of the durian and extracted a sample for me in order to reassure me that it was ripe and tasty. Because the price we settled on was high I asked him to cut a sample from the others in the bunch. 'Not necessary', he replied, 'Satu pohon!' which, translated from Indonesian, means 'one tree' — in other words, the durian all came from the same tree and if one was good, then the rest were certain to be good as well. The man was right and he had touched on a profound biblical truth.

In the Sermon on the Mount Jesus taught, 'Likewise every good tree bears good fruit, but a bad tree bears bad fruit. A good tree cannot bear bad fruit, and a bad tree cannot bear good fruit' (Matt. 7:17-18). Jesus was teaching about the centrality of obedience. In a series of contrasts he distinguishes the genuine disciple from the spurious. The person who follows Jesus as Lord must do more than simply confess his lordship; he must do the will of the Father (Matt. 7:21-23) and put into practice Jesus' words (Matt. 7:24-27). Faith is not simply something to be thought and talked about, but must be incorporated into practice and lived out. This is the burden of the second part of James' letter. In the first part he has laid out a pattern for the growth of faith through testing by trials. In the second part he argues that real faith always issues in deeds and this is the singular mark of Christian growth and maturity.

## The practice of righteousness

What is Christian living all about? When Jesus was asked to summarize what God requires of us, his people, he said that it was loving God and loving our neighbour (Matt. 22:35-40). Christian living is about personal relationships — with God and with others. It is easy to debate the doctrines of the Christian faith, the differences between Catholic and Protestant, the nature of the Trinity, the appropriateness of baptizing children, or perhaps current ethical issues such as abortion and homosexuality, and to think that holding correct views on these matters is the very essence of Christianity. Important as they are, our relationship to Jesus Christ is primarily worked out in the more mundane, less exciting arena of interaction with others.

This new section is signalled by the affectionate address, **'my dear brothers'**, and in it James begins to describe the nature of **'the righteous life that God desires'** (1:20). He introduces the kind of life that pleases God by way of three contrasts — one between hearing and speaking, one between man's anger and God's righteousness and one between rejecting evil and accepting the Word of God. Let us consider each of these in turn.

## A contrast between hearing and speaking (1:19)

Henry Ford was an expert at producing cars, and the corporation he founded is still one of the biggest car manufacturers in the world. But Ford made a mistake early on in his career that cost him millions. One could buy his Model T Ford in any colour one wanted — as long as it was black! The problem was that his customers wanted different colours, but Ford *would not listen*. As a result his competitors gained much of Ford's market share.

Sometimes we are not good listeners because we do not think we have much to learn. We may presume we understand where a person is coming from and what he or she might be thinking or feeling, but good relationships begin with a determination to listen. Good listening is the first step towards the righteous life that God desires. And we are not just to listen; we are to be **'quick to listen'**. Too often we are quick only to speak our minds, or to criticize, or to lay blame and avoid responsibility.

But to whom, or to what, should we be listening? Is it the Word of God? James does not actually tell us. Although we should listen to the Word of God, and that would be a natural application here in view of the context (see 1:18,22-25), nevertheless the kind of listening he is referring to is more general. Otherwise, the following and parallel expression

**'slow to speak'** would also need to refer to God's Word, which would make little sense.

A willingness to listen and restrained speech would go a long way towards solving most of our relationship problems. Together they would dramatically improve communication by showing respect, humility and wisdom. No worthwhile learning or spiritual growth takes place while our mouths are open and our ears are closed. The book of Proverbs connects hearing and speaking in a similar fashion: 'He who answers before listening — that is his folly and his shame' (Prov. 18:13). There are additional benefits as well, since Proverbs teaches that being 'slow to speak' generates a reputation for wisdom even when this is unwarranted: 'Even a fool is thought wise if he keeps silent, and discerning if he holds his tongue' (Prov. 17:28).

## A contrast between man's anger and God's righteousness (1:19-20)

Some cultures are very sensitive to the damaging power of anger. While living in West Java I had to learn the importance of self-control. The Javanese are trained from infancy to avoid encounters that might cause loss of face. It is ingrained in their culture that people give the answer a person wants to hear, lest disappointment lead to anger. It is an almost unimaginable disgrace to lose one's temper publicly. I learned for example never to ask leading questions — never to ask, 'Is this the bus to Jakarta?' The answer would necessarily be 'yes', irrespective of where the bus was going, because that was the answer expected. This was not a deliberate act of falsehood, but to make the other person feel good. The subsequent bus ride to a place I did not want to go to was an opportunity to reflect on **'the righteous life that**

**God desires'** and to learn the importance of being **'slow to become angry'** (1:20).

By contrast, in Western culture public displays of anger are not considered so deplorable. But, whether we are powder kegs or slow burners, **'man's anger'** will keep us from knowing the righteous life that God desires. Indeed, one of the chief reasons for failure in maintaining Christian fellowship is anger. Of course there is a right use of anger. Paul writes, 'Be angry, but do not sin' (Eph. 4:26, RSV). Jesus was angry when God's temple was used as a market-place rather than for prayer, when young children were turned away from him and when religious tradition pre-vented the doing of good on the Sabbath. Nevertheless we need to acknowledge that most of our anger is unrighteous, and the place to take it is the cross.

## Rejecting evil and accepting the word (1:21)

When living in the tropics one must change one's shirt at least once a day. It may be inconvenient, but it is socially necessary. Getting rid of soiled clothing is a word-picture used by James (and also by Paul in Ephesians 4:22,25) to illustrate how we grow spiritually. We must be prepared to **'get rid of all moral filth and the evil that is so prevalent'**. This is a picture of repentance which, while associated with the beginnings of the Christian life, is also a lifelong process. The older we are, the better our repenting should be.

Getting rid of sin is only one part of the growth process. An equally important aspect is to **'humbly accept the word planted in you'**. While the metaphor changes to an agricul-tural one, the idea goes back to the promise in the Old Testament of a new covenant, in which God would one day put his law in the hearts and minds of his people (Jer. 31:31-34). The word planted within the heart is that promise fulfilled — the word of the gospel. But, as the gospel word takes root and grows in the heart, care is required because we have enemies which seek to destroy the word. Opposition comes from the world, the flesh and the devil. These all conspire together to make that word **'which can save you'** prove unfruitful (Mark 4:1-20).

Humility is the essential quality that must accompany the reception of the word. Yet humility is an elusive virtue. If we think we are humble, we are not. I am reminded of the story of the man who wrote a book entitled *Humility and how I obtained it*. Those who are genuinely humble are not aware that they are. So what is this humility, and how do we obtain it? The answer is bound up with the first part of this verse. The truly humble person is acutely aware of his sinfulness and looks to God for help, actively seeking to get rid of all his moral filth, while at the same time feeding upon the Word of God, letting it shape his desires, convictions and actions.

Bible commentator George Stulac tells the story of how, as a young man, he attended a conference for Christian students and during one session an opportunity was given for questions. Someone asked, 'What do you do when things go wrong, when other people are hurting you and you yourself are hurt and angry?' The speaker replied, 'Have your daily quiet time.' Stulac recounts that at the time the answer made him very angry. He thought the response was simplistic and completely overlooked the deep hurt obviously felt by the questioner. Yet later he came to see the wisdom of it. Regular, systematic and prayerful study of God's Word may just be the solution to some of the struggles we face. The simple things are often the hardest for us to accept. In our pride they appear to be an insult to our intelligence. Yet, as James says, we are to 'humbly accept the word', because there are no trials in life which come our way for which the Word of God is not adequate and sufficient.

# 8.
# Hearing aids



*Oh! Give me Samuel's ear,*
*The open ear, O Lord,*
*Alive and quick to hear*
*Each whisper of thy word,*
*Like him to answer at thy call,*
*And to obey thee first of all*
(James Drummond Burns, 1823–1864).

One reason for attending a Bible study is to know the Scriptures better. This is a good step to take. God's Word is not always easy to understand. We can pick it up and read it and not get very much from it at all. Historical distance, cultural change and theological vocabulary all contribute to the difficulties we may face in grasping what is written. We may find ourselves in the position of the Ethiopian who, on his journey home from Jerusalem, could not make head or tail of the writings of the Old Testament prophet Isaiah (Acts 8:26-40). When Philip joined him and asked, 'Do you understand what you are reading?' he replied, 'How can I … unless someone explains it to me?' Perhaps we have felt like this about the Bible.

But there is a pressing reason for engaging in serious examination of the Bible. The God who created all things and gives meaning to his creation has revealed himself in the Scriptures to those who do not know him, or indeed want to know him. Only in the Bible do we learn exactly how God has acted in history to bring men and women, alienated by sin, back to himself through the work of his Son, Jesus Christ. The Bible provides a written, unique, authoritative and interpretative account of what God has done to normalize relations with himself. Therefore the content of this book is crucial to knowing and experiencing God. Yet at this point many fall short of what is required, for it is not sufficient simply to hear (and learn) what the Bible says. In this section James explains why not.

**The principle** (1:22)

Something James has already said could easily be misunderstood. In verse 21 he wrote about the need to 'accept the word planted in you'. This could be interpreted as just listening to God's Word, so he cautions his readers not to **'merely listen to the word, and so deceive yourselves'**. What it really means 'to accept the word' is a listening that is accompanied by obedience: **'Do what it says.'** This is the main idea of verses 22-25.

James is fully committed to the study of Scripture (or listening, as he calls it), but he does caution against a wrong kind of listening. He pictures two kinds of people who come to Bible study, placing them side by side as a contrasting pair. This is a technique he has used before. He has already contrasted the pairs of faith and doubt (1:6), poor and rich (1:9,10), light and shadow (1:17), hearing and speaking (1:19). This teaching method is helpful because, just as black stands out against white better than against grey, it helps us to see differences more readily and to understand and respond.


## Mirror, mirror on the wall (1:23-24)

Much is made of the fact that mirrors in the ancient world were not manufactured from glass, as is the case today, but from polished bronze or copper. The reflections from these metallic mirrors were imperfect, and the imperfect reflection could be the point of the illustration in these verses. The imperfect image of who we are is to be compared with a true likeness of ourselves given by 'the perfect law that gives freedom' (1:25). Indeed, support for this line of thinking seems to come from the only other reference in the New Testament to a mirror. There Paul says, 'Now we see but a poor reflection as in a mirror...' (1 Cor. 13:12). The point Paul makes is based upon the imperfect image produced by the mirror.

But, however attractive this line of interpretation might be, it is almost certainly not the one that James intends here. The mirror that is looked into by each of the two hearers is the same. In both cases it is God's Word. The point that is developed is not so much about *what we see* in the mirror (and we do see something, as we shall observe shortly) as about *what happens afterwards*. One hearer looks and then does something about what he sees. The other looks and then goes away and forgets what he sees. One is blessed by doing, while the other, by merely looking, is self-deceived.

This apt illustration describes the action of someone who looks at his face (literally 'the face of his birth') in the mirror of God's Word, which, among other things, represents to us the truth about ourselves. By nature we are all inclined to think more highly of ourselves than we should. Until brought before the majesty and holiness of God, as we are in Scripture, we are seldom aware of how far we fall short of his glory. Until we encounter the love and mercy of God in Christ, we scarcely comprehend our own spiritual poverty. It is sobering to notice that those who encounter God perceive themselves in a new way and are shaken by the experience. Isaiah saw the Lord in the temple and cried, 'Woe to me!' (Isa. 6:5). When Peter looked into the face of the incarnate Word beside the Sea of Galilee he responded, 'Go away from me, Lord; I am a sinful man!' (Luke 5:8).

Looking at ourselves in the mirror of Scripture can be an uncomfortable experience. Yet we must do so, and we must not think to apply what we see to anyone else, but only to ourselves. Kierkegaard once said, 'When you read God's word you must remember to say to yourself incessantly: It is *I* to whom it is speaking; It is *I* about whom it is speaking.'

However, says James, there is a hearer who takes only a casual glance at the mirror of Scripture and who does not think through its implications and applications. Distractions or busyness undermine serious reflection on what he sees. The result of this kind of behaviour is inevitably superficial. What is read or heard is quickly forgotten.

Forgetfulness is a common fault. Our memories begin to decline in our mid-thirties and by our fifties the deterioration becomes noticeable. We forget people's names, even those of our own children! We pause in mid-sentence because we have lost our train of thought, and words like 'what's-its-name' or 'thingumajig' become a part of our everyday vocabulary. But the forgetting that James writes of is not a degeneracy of the brain; it is a spiritual defect. It is caused by a failure to give Scripture the thought, attention and priority it deserves. Though it is true that a good memory is always an advantage when it comes to any kind of study, the issue here is the condition of the heart, namely its motives and concerns.

**A better kind of Bible study** (1:25)

James sets out a pattern for the person who wants to receive blessing from Bible study.

*1. He gives careful attention to 'the perfect law that gives freedom'*

We are told that 'the word of truth' (1:18), described a little later as 'the word planted in you' (1:21), is also **'the perfect law that gives freedom'** (1:25). This is a reminder of the multifaceted nature of Scripture. The fact that it is the **'perfect law'** reminds us that the coming of Jesus, who interpreted and supplemented the Old Testament law, has brought God's law to mature ('perfect') expression. The description of it as a law **'that gives freedom'** is a reminder that the coming of Jesus fulfilled the Old Testament promise that God would write his law on the hearts of his people (Jer. 31:31-34) and that the accompanying work of the Holy Spirit would make obedience a liberating experience. The believer gives careful attention to this perfect law not because he desires something in return, nor out of fear — because the law no longer condemns — but out of love, because God first loved us.

*2. He continues to do this*

The verb **'continues'** reminds us that fruitful Bible study must be an ongoing endeavour. The discovering and doing of God's will are a never-ending process. Every reading brings fresh discoveries and challenges from God's Word. Renewal is not a once-for-all experience. We need continually to re-form our thinking, attitudes and relationships by returning to Scripture again and again. We need to be convicted afresh of sinful practices, of the poverty of our service, of the ways we can advance in love and holiness. Perfection will never be achieved before the coming of the Lord, yet there is a lifetime of opportunity for progress. The Protestant Reformers spoke of the need to be 'always reforming' (*Semper reformanda est*). This applies not just to the church as a whole, but to its individual members. A casual approach to the Scriptures can never yield anything but superficial discipleship.

*3. He does not forget what he has heard, but puts it into practice*

In our study of Scripture we should expect to be challenged. The letter of James is full of commands (fifty-five of them in 108 verses) that require change and action. We need to be on the lookout for new ways to put into practice what we learn. It may be an apology we need to make, a neighbour to help, a gift to send to a missionary, a child to sponsor, or a habit to break. Knowledge is no substitute for obedience; neither is talking a substitute for doing. No Bible study or sermon can be effective without a serious attempt to apply it. At the same time we should remember that the sheer number of exhortations in James might crush us unless we return again and again to the gospel.

The warning about not being doers of the word is reminiscent of the parable of the two builders (Matt. 7:21-27). John Stott writes on this parable that:

... professing Christians (both the genuine and the spurious) often look alike. You cannot easily tell which is which. Both appear to be building Christian lives. For Jesus is not contrasting professing Christians with non-Christians who make no profession. On the contrary, what is common to both spiritual house builders is that they hear these words of mine (Christ's). So both are members of the visible Christian community. Both read the Bible, go to church, listen to sermons and buy Christian literature. The reason you often cannot tell the difference between them is that the deep foundations of their lives are hidden from view. The real question is not whether they hear Christ's teaching (nor even whether they respect or believe it), but whether they do what they hear. Only a storm will reveal the truth. Sometimes a storm of crisis or calamity betrays what manner of person we are, for 'true piety is not fully distinguished from its counterfeit till it comes to the trial'. If not, the storm of the day of judgement will certainly do so.[1]

## 4. *He will be blessed in what he does*

Do we find blessing in our study of the Bible? Do we feel excitement and expectancy when we open the sacred page? The gospel is never just words; it is God's words. In the Bible we have an authentic encounter with the Lord Jesus Christ. Here is a promise of rich blessing when we practise what we learn.

While it is true that this book was written as an aid to Bible study, the danger of 'doing' Bible study is that this can become a substitute for 'doing' and we can end up having a purely recreational knowledge of God and his Word. It could happen that, even after a lifetime of Bible study, we have never read the Bible correctly. Our knowledge may have grown; our grasp of the great doctrines of the faith may have expanded; we may be able to articulate clearly what we believe, and yet God's Word could still be something impersonal, interesting but not confronting, a topic for discussion and debate that has little impact on the way we live. This is what it means to look *at* God's mirror rather than look *into* it. This is to praise the mirror for its beauty but to fail to recognize the voice of God speaking.

# 9.
# Give me that old-time religion

*Please read James 1:26-27*

Charles Spurgeon is remembered as one of the great nineteenth-century preachers of the evangelical faith. His sermons were printed weekly, and countless thousands have been helped through them. Yet Spurgeon's Christianity was not just talk. He engaged in the building of homes and shelters for orphans and widows. On one occasion when challenged about his beliefs, he reminded his unbelieving critic of the failure of the secular organizations of his day to help the poor and vulnerable. He closed his argument by paraphrasing the words of Elijah at Mount Carmel: 'The God who answers by orphanages, let him be God!'

Just as the righteousness of God which saves us is revealed in the gospel, so too is the righteous life that flows from it. This righteous life counts, not to vindicate faith, but to verify it. Gospel belief and gospel life go hand in hand, precept with practice.

The structure of these two verses is relatively simple. Verse 26 explains that unrestrained speech is symptomatic of a false claim to be religious. Verse 27 tells us that genuine religion consists of caring for the weak and vulnerable, as well as distancing ourselves from the mindset and lifestyle of the world. Even though we may not take these verses as providing a comprehensive description of the religious life, they form a crucial part of it.

## Restraining the tongue (1:26)

'Religion' is a negative word for many Christians, who construe it in terms of man's efforts to get in touch with deity. According to this definition, the religious person does all the work and offers it to God, expecting him to receive it and reward accordingly. But this is a self-help approach to acceptance with God and, as such, contrary to the gospel, which makes it plain that God takes the initiative in reaching out to sinners. He provides forgiveness and salvation in the cross of Christ and offers it freely to all who receive it by faith alone.

James, however, uses the word **'religion'** in another sense, as the practice of faith (the same word is found in Acts 26:5 and Col. 2:18). In that sense we are all **'religious'** because we all *do* something on the basis of what we believe. Verse 26 presents us with the case of a practising Christian who fails to restrain his tongue. However, the world's best religious practice counts for nothing where there is a lack of self-control in speech. That kind of religion is, says James, **'worthless'**.

Careless use of the tongue is a common theme in Scripture. It is indicative of the widespread and sometimes catastrophic failure in this area of the religious life:

He who guards his lips guards his life,
    but he who speaks rashly will come to ruin
                                        (Prov. 13:3).


But I tell you that men will have to give account on
the day of judgement for every careless word they

have spoken. For by your words you will be acquitted, and by your words you will be condemned (Matt. 12:36-37).

The tongue also is a fire, a world of evil among the parts of the body. It corrupts the whole person, sets the whole course of his life on fire, and is itself set on fire by hell (James 3:6).

The picture used to describe the need for control is that of a bridle (see also 3:2-3). The bridle attaches to a metal bit which is placed in the horse's mouth, giving the rider control of his mount's behaviour and direction. The use of a bridle to check the horse can be painful, but without it the rider's safety is in jeopardy because he cannot guide or control the animal.

Words do have a great deal of power. Misuse of them can cause much hurt. When we are unduly quick to criticize, or to dismantle someone else's reputation, or too ready to cast doubt on the orthodoxy of others, then we are setting ourselves up as experts on the religious life. We might think we are exercising good judgement and discernment, but in reality we are showing that our religion is worthless. The unchecked tongue betrays a deep-seated malaise. The disturbing aspect of this sin is our capacity to simultaneously engage in it and still believe in the value of our service for Christ.

The person who cannot control his speech **'deceives himself'**. Life gives many examples of our capacity to fool ourselves. We see self-deception in the alcoholic who cannot admit to a drinking problem, or the patient in denial over a life-threatening illness, or the parent who cannot accept that his (or her) child is telling a lie. The issue of self-deception over imprudent speech poses a greater threat to religious people because the stakes are so much higher.

## Caring for the needy (1:27)

Religion that is acceptable to God is not explained in terms of institutions (churches, denominations), ritual (worship, liturgy) or books (Bible, hymnal). While these have a place, religion is in fact the application of faith to life. Thus our collective worship on a Sunday only has meaning as it reflects the practice of our faith carried out through the week (Rom. 12:1).

True religion is described first by two ethical qualities, **'pure'** and **'faultless'**, which are then expanded to provide a concrete example of what they might mean in reality: **'to look after orphans and widows...'** For a Jewish reader both terms, when used in a religious context, meant keeping the outward, ritual sacrifices and washings prescribed by the law in order to open up access to God. In the Gospels Jesus taught that the externals of religion are not enough; purity of heart and life are what count (Matt. 23:25-26; Luke 11:39-41). **'Faultless'** (better rendered 'undefiled') is the negative expression of the positive quality of purity. A pure and faultless religion might suggest some ethereal, rare kind of piety possessed by only a few, but the down-to-earth description that follows brings it within the reach of every believer.

Ministry to orphans and widows has a long and noble tradition in Scripture because God takes a special interest in their cause (Exod. 22:22; Deut. 10:18; 14:29; 24:17; Ps. 146:9; Isa. 1:17). Indeed God describes himself as a 'father to the fatherless' (Ps. 68:5), which may be the origin for the combined title of **'God'** with **'our Father'** used in this verse.

**'Orphans and widows'** were those who were defenceless and at risk in ancient societies. By mentioning only orphans and widows, however, James is not giving us a comprehensive list of those deserving our special attention, but rather a representative one. Today that might mean giving assistance to people regardless of belief, gender, race or ethnic background, perhaps by supporting a family following a multiple birth, driving an elderly person to a medical appointment, sponsoring a child, and so on. The list of possibilities is endless.

We have a responsibility to help the helpless **'in their distress'**. The root meaning of the word is a pressure which can be either spiritual or material. Even though we have many legitimate needs, such as food, clothing and shelter, the most basic of all human needs is reconciliation with the Father through the gospel of our Lord Jesus Christ. No dichotomy exists in Scripture between the gospel and its social consequences. This is because God is the God of nature as well as the God of spirit. He is concerned for the whole of life — body and soul.

Nevertheless the deeper reason we should engage in ministry to 'orphans and widows' is because of God's love for us. At one time we were helpless. We had become fatherless through sin. Jesus was sent in order that we might know God as Father through his Son. No other act of God shows his identification with the plight of the weak more than the giving of Christ. His identification with us led him to death on the cross, the supreme act of costly love. And no other basis exists for our present status as the children of God. To the extent that we have experienced the power of Calvary love, to that degree we shall find ourselves compelled to care for 'orphans and widows in their distress'.

## Keeping our distance (1:27)

The other element of religion that is pure and faultless before God is keeping **'oneself from being polluted by the world'**. Notice the careful balance. Practical care for the needy of the world must be accompanied by vigilance against the influence of the world.

This is the first time James mentions **'the world'** and he does so as a negative factor in the quest for Christian maturity. Later in the letter we shall study in more detail the way that James describes both the problems that the world causes (4:1-6) and the remedy for them (4:7-10). In this verse he merely draws our attention to the polluting power of the world.

The 'world' James writes of has a sinister ring to it. It is the inhabited world which God created to reflect his glory, but which sin entered into and which is now organized in rebellion against him. Hostile to his rule, the world actively hates Jesus and those who belong to him (John 15:18). As defined by John, the world is characterized by the quest for pleasure, profit and power (1 John 2:15-17). Though this is the world we live in at present, we must not allow it to live in us.

The world has a corrupting power on the believer; therefore separation from it is required. The separation is not social. We are to identify with the world in its need (for example, by visiting orphans and widows), but not in its pride and hostility to God. Keeping oneself from being polluted is dissociation from the world's values, not from the world's people. In the words of Iain Murray:

> Worldliness is departing from God. It is a man-centred way of thinking; it proposes objectives which demand no radical breach with man's fallen nature; it judges the importance of things by the present and material results; it weighs success by numbers; it covets human esteem and wants no unpopularity; it knows no truth for which it is worth suffering; it declines to be a 'fool for Christ's sake'. Worldliness is the mindset of

the unregenerate. It adopts idols and is at war with God.[1]

Pollution has become one of the major social and political issues of our time. 'Climate change', 'global warming', 'carbon trading', 'greenhouse gases', 'ozone depletion' and other phrases are all part of a new vocabulary associated with pollution of the environment. Green is the symbolic colour used by environmental groups and political parties who want to protect our physical world. In Scripture that colour is white, symbolizing moral and spiritual purity (e.g. Isa. 1:18; Ps. 51:7). The dominant pollutants are pride, because man will not accept God's rule, and covetousness, because in seeking to gratify his lusts he worships them (Col. 3:5). Where we have become polluted by the world we have a wonderful recourse in Christ our Saviour, who, by his sacrifice on the cross, can cleanse us from our sin and make us white again.

# 10.
# Keeping the faith without favouritism



*Please read James 2:1-4*

Impartiality is the essential quality in a judge. Indeed justice is sometimes represented as a blindfolded woman holding a pair of scales. The blindfold symbolizes a lack of prejudice. She does not see the parties before her and therefore cannot show favouritism. She simply hears and must make a decision based solely on the evidence presented. Favouritism takes place where one person is treated differently from another, on the basis of wealth, social status, gender, age, or physical appearance.

Impartiality is important for relationships. 'Not fair!' cry children, who are quick to imagine bias in a parent towards a brother or sister. In the classroom a student is called a teacher's pet when preferential attention is given. A sporting referee who makes inconsistent decisions is greeted with howls of protest. We all love and expect to be treated with equity. But does this happen in our churches? This is the issue raised now by James.

But what, if any, are the connections between this new topic of favouritism and what has been written previously? Perhaps James intends us to see an example of the polluting power of the world (1:27) in the bias displayed towards the rich man (2:1-4). 'The deceitfulness of wealth' created distinctions in the church which grace had once removed. Care for the poor, not discrimination against them, is a mark of religion that God our Father accepts (1:27). When distinctions are made on the basis of wealth, the law, which ought to be heard and acted on, is violated (1:25; 2:9). The existence of rich and poor together in the church is one of the trials appointed by God for our growth in maturity (1:2-4).

What was the original situation that called forth this command not to show favouritism? It has nearly always been assumed that the setting in these verses is that of a regular church meeting for worship. The wealthy visitor enters the place of assembly and one of the ushers (perhaps with the tacit consent of other members — **'you'** is plural) conducts him to a comfortable seat in a prominent position. By contrast the man who is not well off, as evidenced by his shabby attire, is treated with contempt. Some recent writers have questioned this scenario and argued instead that the setting is that of a judicial hearing to settle a case between two church members. Certainly the language used is legal; James also warns those who are judges not to find in favour of the wealthy on the basis of outward appearances, and there is a reference in verse 6 to a court case. But that is as far as the evidence takes us. It is hard to be dogmatic when there is little specific information. On balance the traditional interpretation seems better because seating arrangements are more likely to be the basis of favouritism in a worship setting than in a legal one.

## Favouritism — inconsistent with faith (2:1)

The appeal to **'my brothers'** is especially noteworthy. It is a powerful reminder that if we are brothers it is because God has made no distinctions among us. Wealth, position, appearance, or any other advantage we may have possessed, had no influence on God. In fact nothing mattered except that Jesus Christ graciously intervened to draw us to himself. When he looked upon us in our poverty he spoke kindly and said, 'Here's a good seat for you' (2:3), and we were added to his family and his church.

The church should be the only community in this world where the age-old dream of philosophers and politicians of forging an equitable and just society begins to be realized. The word 'brothers' means that a relationship has been established between us by God. We cannot see it; we may not even feel naturally drawn to all our brethren; but the relationship is there all the same. We belong to the same family, bound by ties that are spiritual and eternal.

The warmth of the address is followed by a warning against inconsistent behaviour: **'As believers … don't show favouritism'** (2:1). The literal translation is in fact, 'Don't show favouritisms' (note the plural), suggesting that, even though the illustration that follows is specific to wealth, the application is far wider. Affluence is not the only cause of favouritism, which may be based on superficial qualities, such as the colour of skin, looks, dress, health, age, sex, level of education, authority, influence, position, popularity, and so on. James is not talking about friendships. He is not saying friendships are bad. He is referring to our treatment of people in general. To pay attention to one group while deliberately ignoring another because they are not my type (or because they are) is wrong.

The reason why favouritism is forbidden is because we have a faith which rests in **'our glorious Lord Jesus Christ'**. The latter title for Jesus is sometimes translated 'our Lord Jesus Christ, *the Lord* of glory' (KJV, TEV). The repetition of the word 'Lord' (in italics) covers the uncertainty as to how the word 'glory' relates to Jesus. Either way, this is an unusual description of Jesus. Not only is it rare for James to mention the name of Christ explicitly (only here and in 1:1), but this description is found nowhere else in Scripture. So why does he draw our attention in particular to Jesus Christ as the Lord of glory?

We might begin to answer by exploring the word 'glory', which signifies both the splendour of God and the place of his abode. While it is true that Jesus is glorious, possessing the same splendour that God does, there are good reasons for supposing that James is thinking of glory as the place where God dwells. Glory is where Jesus is now exalted and rules over all, and from whence he will come again as the Judge (5:9). But, and this is more pertinent to the context, glory is also the place from which Jesus came down to save us. He showed no partiality when it came to rescuing poor helpless sinners. He did not look at the shabby clothes of our attempted righteousness and choose to ignore us. Rather:

> … taking the very nature of a servant,
> being made in human likeness.
> And being found in appearance as a man,
> he humbled himself
> and became obedient to death — even death on a
> cross
>
> (Phil. 2:7-8).

He exchanged heaven's highest glory for life among us in our broken world.

During his earthly ministry Jesus had no favourites. He was equally at home in the presence of wealthy men like Zacchaeus and in the humble abode of Lazarus. He ate with tax collectors and sinners as well as in the home of the Pharisee. Even his enemies recognized his impartiality. They acknowledged that 'You do not show partiality, but teach the way of God in accordance with the truth' (Luke 20:21). It is true that some of his friends, such as Peter, James and John, were closer to him than others, but there was no favouritism.

In fact, when they deserved it, those same men received some of his most severe rebukes (Matt. 16:23; Luke 9:55).

Showing partiality is a contradiction of faith in Christ, who did not show partiality in coming down from glory to save us, poor as we are. Though it may be detected in the home, school, workplace, or even in the judicial system, in the church it is a fundamental denial of the gospel of grace. If the church does not wipe out partiality, then partiality will wipe out the church.

## Favouritism — illustrated from wealth (2:2-3)

'Goldfinger — he's the man, the man with the Midas touch,' sings Shirley Bassey in the James Bond film of the same name. 'Goldfinger' is the literal translation of the word used to describe the man who comes into the Christian assembly here. It is a reference to his brightly coloured clothes and ostentatious show of wealth. He receives preferential treatment in contrast to the poor man, whose clothes are **'shabby'** — perhaps mismatched, frayed and in need of a wash. Bias towards the rich over the poor is a widespread evil. Too often in church circles money does the talking. Although the illustration given is hypothetical (**'Suppose a man comes**...') yet, from what follows ('But you have insulted the poor...'), something like it seems to have already happened.

We might ask why James singles out wealth to illustrate favouritism, and not racial prejudice or intellectual snobbery? The answer may be because the churches to which he wrote were poor and therefore partiality towards the wealthy posed the greatest threat (Rom. 15:26; 1 Cor. 1:26). Lack of income, or a budget crisis, is a recurrent problem for the church treasurer and finance committee. There never seems to be enough money to keep up with the expenses, let alone do what we would like. Hence the temptation to show undue regard to rich people, to defer to their wishes, to be more careful not to give offence that might cause them to be upset, leave and take their patronage (i.e. their money!) with them. By contrast less care may be taken with the single parent, pensioner or unemployed person, all of whom are unable to contribute to the ministry, and who are, indeed, more likely to consume the time and resources of the church.

The **'poor'** are to be evangelized, discipled, taught, cared for and shown the same love as the person who can rescue the church from a budget crisis. To act in any other way is to set up different (what James calls **'evil'**) standards. There needs to be a robust even-handedness in ministry. The illustration calls us to discount social and economic differences that may exist across the members or visitors who attend our meetings. To do otherwise is a denial of the faith we hold and a blatant contradiction of the example given by the Lord who came from the glory.

## Favouritism — challenged by examination (2:4)

James asks the question, **'... have you not discriminated among yourselves, and become judges with evil thoughts?'** Now we are never told that we are to suspend our critical faculties. Nor are we forbidden to have an opinion about someone else. Indeed, we are encouraged at all times to distinguish truth from error, good from evil. Our Lord tells us not to cast pearls before swine (Matt. 7:6) and to watch out for false prophets who come in sheep's clothing (Matt. 7:15). But this is not what Jesus or James mean when they warn against judging with evil thoughts.

We become judges with evil thoughts whenever we pay less attention to, or show lack of courtesy to, the **'poor man'**. It doesn't matter what kind of poverty it is. The poverty may be that of beauty. The world says, 'You need to be good-looking', because with beauty you can have money, admirers and respect. Life then becomes a Darwinian struggle where only the beautiful win out. It may be a poverty of personality, so that lack of charisma makes us uninterested in another. It may be that someone is 'poor' in terms of influence, so that they can be of no advantage to us and therefore can be safely ignored. It may be that someone wears dowdy, unfashionable clothes.

When factors like these determine our relationships with people, we have not understood the heart of God, or the nature of the faith we profess. The way we treat others is a test of maturity (1:2-4) and a daily battle for integrity.

When Jesus came to his own, he turned upside down the norms of this world. The first becomes last; he who exalts himself is humbled; the greatest becomes a servant. The poor in spirit are blessed and the meek inherit the earth. He created a new society where all discrimination is dissolved (Gal. 3:28). The church must be the one place where it does not matter what your standing in life is. Each person should receive love, respect and consideration, and his or her worth should not be determined by any external quality. James picks up on this glorious vision of the church that Jesus gave. In this new society the unsung and the unlovely find a home. They are accepted because God in Christ has accepted them.

# 11.
# Why favouritism is wrong

*Please read James 2:5-13*

James allocates a surprising amount of space to the unequal treatment of rich and poor in the church, which at the very least should signal the importance of the topic for us. Verses 5-13 add three further reasons why favouritism brings the gospel into disrepute. A fawning subservience towards the rich and a disregard of the poor fail, firstly, to understand the choice God makes; secondly, are irrational in view of the behaviour of the rich; and, thirdly, break the royal law.

**Favouritism is contrary to God's choice of the poor**
**(2:5-6)**

Selina, Countess of Huntingdon, was a great supporter of the Evangelical Revival of the eighteenth century, using her position and wealth to sponsor the spread of the gospel and care of the poor. She used to say that she had been 'saved by an "m"'. Paul writes to the Corinthians, 'Brothers, think of what you were when you were called. Not *many* of you were wise by human standards; not *many* were influential; not *many* were of noble birth' (1 Cor. 1:26, italics added). He does not say 'not *any*' were noble, but 'not *many*'. Lady

Selina was acutely aware that the greater number of those God chooses, calls and saves are those who are unremarkable in the world's eyes.

This is the point of verse 5, which is put as a question, **'Has not God chosen those who are poor in the eyes of the world to be rich in faith ...?'**, but is phrased so as to anticipate the answer 'Yes'. In other words, God's choice of the poor is an undeniable truth. God has honoured the **'poor in the eyes of the world'** by extending his grace to so many of them. To discriminate against them is to contradict the will of God. It is to go against what is so evident in the kind of people whom God chooses to add to his church. Notice that the appeal concerns the action of God. What we know about God, and not mere morality, undergirds the call for change.

Someone might object and say, 'But this is reverse discrimination; God is discriminating against the wealthy.' The objection would be false and a slur on God, for Scripture is clear that God is equitable in all his dealings, does not show bias and is not swayed by external appearances (Deut. 10:17; 2 Chr. 19:7; Acts 10:34; Rom. 2:11; Eph. 6:9; Col. 3:25; 1 Peter 1:17). It would also be untrue, for God does include the wealthy among those he saves (cf. 1:10; 2:21; 5:11). Moreover, we go further than what James intends if we conclude that God rejects the rich. He does not say that God has chosen the poor rather than the rich. He merely contrasts his reader's attitude to, and treatment of, the poor with God's.

The wider testimony of the Scripture is that our standing before God is all on the basis of grace. Neither poverty nor wealth count for anything in the kingdom of God. But if wealth causes someone to become self-satisfied and self-sufficient, and consequently to reject salvation, God cannot be held responsible. And if poverty causes another to experience discrimination and helps him to a whole-hearted response to God's gift of love, it is to his praise.

Why are many Christians poor? Undoubtedly many of the early Christians were poor when God saved them and remained so because of persecution. Some suffered loss of personal possessions (Heb. 10:34); others were forced out of their homes (Acts 8:1). Today Christians in the West little realize how costly it is to follow Christ in many parts of the world. Our brethren face daily discrimination from neighbours, employers and governments, yet the Lord has a special place for those whom the world despises.

**Favouritism doesn't make sense** (2:6-7)

The second reason given for not showing favouritism towards the rich is because of their behaviour. Paying undue attention to them is senseless because it is they **'who are exploiting you'**, says James. This is not a call to be unkind to the rich because they have been unkind to the poor. Retaliation is not a Christian ethic. A fawning attitude to the rich to obtain special favour is a grave error of judgement and flies in the face of the harsh treatment they give out to believers. Some of the first readers were poor because of the corrupt practices of the wealthy (e.g. 5:4). The wealthy were often litigious, using the legal system (either its high costs or bribery) to exploit the weak.

**'Are they not the ones who are slandering the noble name of him to whom you belong?'** Blasphemy consists of disrespectful speech, attitudes or actions with respect to God. To blaspheme is to trivialize the sacred. The rich were despising **'the noble name'**. How this took place is not explained. Perhaps it was by mocking Christian worship, or by taking God's name in vain, or slandering the name of Christ.

These arguments show the sheer folly of paying undue attention to the rich when they, by their actions, have shown utter disregard for the church and for Christ.


**Favouritism breaks the royal law** (2:8-11)

Favouritism is wrong because God gave a law in the Old Testament Scripture: **'Love your neighbour as yourself.'** This reference to the law of love (Lev. 19:18) is especially fitting here since in the Old Testament too it is linked by the context with discrimination against the poor (Lev. 19:15).

The law is described as **'royal'**, meaning that it is the law of a king. By this unique description James almost certainly points to Jesus as the ruler of the kingdom which he has **'promised [to] those who love him'** (2:5). It is royal not only because Jesus taught that this command of love acted as a summary of the law in respect of our duty towards our neighbour (Matt. 22:36-40), but also because Jesus personally charged his disciples to keep the command as his own special commandment (John 13:34). Favouritism is therefore especially heinous since it violates the command to love the 'dear brothers'. It is to despise those whom Jesus loves. Keeping this law, on the other hand, shows a maturity which is set forth as the goal of this letter (1:2-4).

James argues that the law is a unity by reference to two of the commandments. Someone has described the law as a sheet of glass rather than a pile of stones. A stone removed from the pile leaves the rest undisturbed, but break the glass and the whole thing is broken. The law is one because the one God gave it. Perhaps in the churches to which James was writing favouritism was regarded as a minor matter and not really a transgression. James responds by proving that favouritism is a contradiction of the law of Christ and is as inconsistent as claiming that adultery is wrong but murder is acceptable (2:11).


**Favouritism will be judged** (2:12-13)

We are to **'speak and act as those who are going to be judged by the law'**. Again present behaviour is determined by the future event of judgement (see also 1:12). Both word and deed together form a genuine expression of faith. The return to the theme of speaking and doing is a reminder that steering clear of favouritism is a valid application of what it means to do what the word says (1:22).

Some Christians claim that the law is now irrelevant. 'Free from the law — Oh, happy condition! I can sin as I like and still find remission!' might describe their attitude. Verse 12 clearly contradicts this view, for we are to **'be judged by the law that gives freedom'**. To be sure, we are not subject to the law for our justification. The law can no longer condemn us, as its demands have been met by Christ's death on the cross. So in what sense are we to be judged by the law of liberty?

The law is liberating when it is used in the manner for which it was intended. The law was never meant to be a stairway to heaven. Indeed, it is a liberating experience to recognize that we do not keep the law to earn salvation. Rather, the law is obeyed because it instructs us in what the Lord wants us to be and to do. We follow its precepts out of a deep sense of gratitude to the one who has redeemed us. In this sense the law is precious, giving joy to those who use it aright (cf. Ps. 19:7-8; 119). It is therefore wrong to pit 'living by the Spirit' against keeping the law as though they were conflicting concepts. The Spirit-filled Christian is precisely the one who seeks to be obedient. Indeed, Jesus commanded our adherence to the law, saying, 'Anyone who breaks one of the least of these commandments and teaches others to do the same will be called least in the kingdom of heaven, but whoever practises and teaches these commands will be called great in the kingdom of heaven' (Matt. 5:19).

John Calvin helpfully comments:

> We ought not to be frightened away from the law or to shun its instruction merely because it requires a much stricter moral purity than we shall reach while we bear about with us the prison house of our body. For the law is not now acting toward us as a rigorous enforcement officer who is not satisfied unless the requirements are met. But in this perfection to which it exhorts us, the law points out the goal toward which throughout life we are to strive... If we fail not in this struggle, it is well. Indeed, this whole life is a race; when its course has been run, the Lord will grant us to attain that goal to which our efforts now press forward from afar.[1]

It is by the law that we are to be judged. This judgement will be one of rewards and losses (1 Cor. 3:14-15; 2 Cor. 5:10). On that future day the quality of mercy — the practical, compassionate treatment of others and whether we have discriminated against the poor, or failed to give help to those in need when it was in our power to do so (2:15-16) — will be a key indicator of the reality of our faith in Christ (cf. Jesus' teaching in Matt. 18:21-35). To fail here and not be merciful, however, is indicative of an unbelieving heart, and so opens us to judgement without mercy.

The last sentence, **'Mercy triumphs over judgement'**, is difficult, since it is not clear whether divine or human mercy is intended. If it is human mercy, then James means that our mercy, while not being the basis of our salvation, is the undeniable evidence of it. And if that is true then we can look in confidence to Christ at the judgement, knowing that he has fulfilled all the claims the law might have on us.

Are we impartial and even-handed, giving proper attention to every brother or sister — to the ones who may never be able to give to the ministry, or the building programme, and who perhaps will take up more time being helped than contributing themselves? Do we make church appointments impartially, without respect of persons, or do the factors of friendship or personal interest sway decisions? Friendship can so easily slide into favouritism of different kinds — cronyism, nepotism etc. — where positions are given because we like a person rather than on merit. Do love, compassion and respect for others, irrespective of external appearances, motivate and guide us? Genuine love for our neighbour is rooted in Christ, who loved us while we were unlovable and sacrificially gave himself for us while we were impoverished.

# 12.
# Faith: dead or alive?

*Please read James 2:14-17*

Faith is so basic to Christianity that we regularly speak of the Christian religion as 'the Christian faith'. Since the sixteenth-century Reformation in particular, Protestants have argued that God accepts and accounts a sinner as righteous before him not because of deeds done, but only because of the merits of Christ. This act of God's free grace is received by faith alone and without regard to anything done, either good or bad. This is the doctrine of justification by faith rediscovered in Scripture by Martin Luther. It brought him and countless others out of the soul-destroying man-centred systems of approaching God that were present in so much of medieval spirituality.

However, the Reformation heritage, with its antipathy towards a works-based righteousness, does lend itself to a misunderstanding about the place of works. We are nervous about deeds in case we fall back into the way of thinking that something which we do could contribute to our salvation. And that is ever a danger. The default setting of the fallen human heart has always been to pride and self-righteousness. But there is another danger, which is to discount the necessary and evidential nature of works as a testimony to the presence of genuine faith. It is this latter concern that James addresses here.

This new section is the cause of some contention over the right of the letter of James to be in the Bible. Because of it Luther described James, in an oft-repeated phrase, as 'an epistle of straw'. He did not like the apparent contradiction between it and Paul's teaching on the relationship between faith and works (e.g. Rom. 3:28). More recently others have criticized James because they think he does not sufficiently move away from the Judaism of his day so as to express clearly the essence of the gospel. And the role of works is still a contentious issue, as seen in the 'New Perspective' debate on Paul, as well as attempts by Protestant and Catholic theologians to reformulate the doctrine of justification in such a way as to roll back four hundred years of sometimes bitter division.

Understanding the connection between faith and works is necessary for Christian maturity (1:2-4). If we grasp this relationship we shall be able to move freely not just through the teaching of this letter, but through all Scripture. Clearly some of James' readers had not understood this relationship and were in danger of going astray. To go astray at this point, however, is to fail completely, for faith that is not accompanied by works (translated as **'deeds'** in the NIV) is **'dead'** — it cannot save (2:17).

**The principle** (2:14)

Twice the question, **'What good is it…?'**, is asked in relation to a person who makes a claim to have a faith which is unsupported by deeds (2:14,16). Of course there is nothing wrong with claiming to have faith. Genuine faith is conceived as something that brings good to the person who exercises it. In fact there is no greater blessing in life than to possess faith in Christ. Faith alone is the means by which we enter into good standing with God and are counted righteous before him (Rom. 3:22); it is the necessary requirement in order to please the Lord (Heb. 11:6); and the Christian life is to be lived by faith from first to last (Rom. 1:17).

However, the following question, **'Can *such* faith save him?'** (italics added), implies that not everything that is called faith is a faith that saves.[1] An imaginary person (**'If one of you says ...'**) makes the claim, perhaps along the lines: 'Works are not necessary — only my faith counts for salvation.' The claim, though presented hypothetically, represents the actual thinking of some.

So what are we to think about someone who says he has faith but does not have works? The claim seems to have merit. Elsewhere in Scripture, and particularly from the apostle Paul, we have statements such as, 'A man is justified by faith apart from observing the law' (Rom. 3:28). Or again, 'For it is by grace you have been saved, through faith — and this not from yourselves, it is the gift of God — not by works, so that no one can boast' (Eph. 2:8-9). The illustration that follows makes clear what is wrong with this 'faith-only' idea.


**The illustration** (2:15-16)

The illustration is about a **'brother or sister'** who is probably not literally **'without clothes'** of any kind, but is in need of warm outer clothing. John uses the same word to describe Peter when he had removed his outer garments for work (John 21:7). To be without **'daily food'** indicates someone who is underfed or malnourished. Faced with this conspicuous need, a church member (**'one of you'**) responds: **'Go, I wish you well; keep warm and well fed,'** yet fails to offer any practical help. Such a faith — one which, though expressed in sympathetic words and warmth of feeling, falls short of action — is dead.

Notice first the misuse of speech, of which James has more to say later (3:1-12). The pious words express affection and blessing but lack conviction and depth and alter nothing. Here is religious language with no moral root. Are any of our meetings just religious talking shops? If in the aftermath of these meetings no practical good is done, are we not deluding ourselves?

The Christian life might be thought of in terms of advances in mission, heroic acts of piety, victories in soul-winning and church growth with dynamic leadership. This is the stuff of hagiography and is adored by the success-driven mentality of many. And the Lord might use his people in the above ways, but, as far as James is concerned, the essence of a vital faith is expressed in a far more mundane way, by seeing a fellow brother or sister in want and meeting their need. While in James' illustration the hardship may be material, his application cannot be limited to material need. There are those whose needs are not visible — the depressed, lonely, stressed, grief-stricken and abused. A living faith instinctively reaches out and serves those needs, and heaven responds: 'Whatever you did for one of the least of these brothers of mine, you did for me' (Matt. 25:40).


**The conclusion** (2:17)


The only kind of faith that saves is one that issues in good works. J. I. Packer has rightly said, 'What saves is faith alone, but the faith that saves is never alone.' It must be added that even the good works we do which are the fruit of saving faith cannot count towards our salvation. In our best moments there is always an admixture of sin and self that cannot withstand the scrutiny of Christ when he comes to judge the world in righteousness. On that day Christ's righteousness alone will be our sufficiency and salvation. Even so, works are the living proof of a vital faith. To the person who claims to have faith, James says, 'Show me the evidence.'

In this respect James is not contradicting Paul. Paul is concerned lest we try to bring any of our works into the equation of righteousness, thinking to raise something alongside the finished and sufficient work of Christ. James, on the other hand, explores the nature of the faith that saves. He gives us an important test by which to gauge whether our faith is real or imagined. If we want to know whether our faith is living, then we need to ask how we are living. Good works are the uniform telltale sign of saving faith.

Paul makes the same point in his letter to the Galatians upon which Gresham Machen comments:

> In Galatians 5:6, he [Paul] says, 'for in Christ Jesus there is neither circumcision nor uncircumcision; but faith working through love.' 'Faith working through love' is the key to an understanding both of Paul and of James. The faith about which Paul has been speaking is not the idle faith which James condemns, but a faith that works. It works itself out through love. And what love is Paul explains in the whole last division of Galatians. It is no mere emotion, but the actual fulfilling of the whole moral law. 'For the whole law is fulfilled in one word, even in this: Thou shalt love thy neighbour as thyself' (Gal. 5:14). Paul is fully as severe as James against a faith that permits men to continue in sin. The faith about which he is speaking is a faith that receives the Spirit who gives men power to lead a holy life.[2]

Finally, with all this discussion on the importance of works, we must not go to the other extreme and think that it is only what we do that matters. Works without faith are as dead as faith without works. James is not calling us to activism. The cutting edge of the kingdom of God is not mere social action to alleviate human suffering without concern for what we believe. Of all the virtues, the faith which rests on Christ is the source of all other Christian graces, and Christ looks for it and honours it.

# 13.
# Grace: 'light and easy'

*Please read James 2:18-26*

Whenever the gospel is proclaimed, objections are inevitably raised: 'What about suffering?' 'Where do people go who have never heard about Jesus?' 'Hasn't science disproved faith?' Some objectors are not interested in the truth, only in fault-finding and argument. Though they may say they have genuine problems in believing, they do not really want answers because they know that commitment to Christ would mean a radical change of thinking and lifestyle. Their problems are not really intellectual, but moral and spiritual. Others have genuine concerns that hinder acceptance of the gospel and growth in grace. They need answers and reasons to believe. James' willingness to clarify the point in verse 18 suggests that this latter kind of person is in view here.

The goal of maturity (1:2-4) can be achieved not only by giving positive instruction, but also by removing barriers to it. James now removes one such barrier by answering a hypothetical yet nevertheless important objection: **'But someone will say ...'** (compare a similar approach by Paul in Rom. 9:19; 1 Cor. 15:35). While we cannot simply reason people towards maturity, wrong-headed thinking does hinder growth. James does not only aim to correct our thinking; he also wants to challenge us to action. The objection revisits the relationship between faith and works introduced previously, though in a fresh way. In the previous section (2:14-17) the religious person equated faith with *feelings*; in this section the person equates faith with *thinking*.

What precisely is the objection, and to what mindset is James responding? There is no easy answer to this question and little agreement among Bible scholars. Indeed, this section has been called (by Dibelius) 'one of the most difficult New Testament passages in general'. The NIV makes the objection: **'You have faith; I have deeds'** (cf. NKJV, RSV). This rendering is possible since the earliest Greek manuscripts had very little in the way of punctuation. It is also a natural reading of the text and assumes that the imaginary objector was arguing against James' insistence that deeds were the necessary evidence of faith. But if this is correct it would have made more sense for the objector to put it the other way round and say, 'You [James] have deeds; I [the objector] have faith.' The challenge could, of course, come from a supporter of James. However, James goes on to call the objector a **'foolish man'** (2:20) — hardly the way to address someone who is on your side!

An alternative approach is to alter the objection by extending it to include all of verse 18: 'But someone may well say, "You have faith and I have works; show me your faith without the works, and I will show you my faith by my works"' (NASB). However, similar difficulties to those outlined above still remain. The pronouns 'you' and 'I' make better sense when applied to James and the objector respectively.

One solution is to make the 'you' and the 'I' indefinite and to understand that James is simply making a general reference, as he did with the previous objection (2:14). This solution is adopted by at least one modern translation: 'But someone will say, "One person has faith, another has actions"' (TEV). Although it is not an exact rendering of the personal pronouns, on balance this is probably the best option.

Rather than trying to work out exactly how the objection is stated, we are on firmer ground in determining James' view of the relationship of faith to deeds (translated as 'works' in other versions of the Bible) when we examine his response rather than the objection, which is that:

- Works demonstrate real faith (2:18).
- Profession of faith, even if doctrinally correct, is insufficient (2:19).
- Faith apart from works is useless (2:20) and dead (2:26).
- Old Testament characters like Abraham and Rahab prove the vital connection between faith and works (2:21-25).

The objector seems to understand faith as something purely intellectual — that merely believing certain truths about God means we are in a right standing with him. Further, the objector considers works as an optional extra — perhaps a gift that some have but others do not. James will have none of this. Such an understanding of faith, he responds, is so defective that even the demons can be said to share it.


**The example of demonic faith** (2:19)

Genuine faith comprises three elements:

*1. Knowledge*

I need to understand the basic facts of the Christian faith — namely that God is the Creator of all things, that I am estranged from him by sin and under his wrath, and that he has sent his Son as Saviour to a fallen world. I need to know the content of the gospel before I can respond to it.

## 2. Agreement

I need not only to know, but also to agree with the gospel, in the sense that I believe it to be true. I agree that God is one, that I am fallen and separated from God by sin, and that Christ is the eternal Son of God who died on the cross as a punishment for my sin.

## 3. Trust

I need to have a personal trust in, reliance on, and commitment to Christ as my Saviour and Lord. This response to the gospel is life-changing as I seek to bring my life into obedience to his will and word.

The mistake the objector makes is to regard faith as no more than the *knowledge* and *agreement* described above. James congratulates him for at least making a good beginning: **'You believe that there is one God. Good!'** The objector correctly understands and agrees with the basic truth that there is one God. James quotes the affirmation (called the Shema) that every orthodox Jew would recite daily (Deut. 6:4-9). To be orthodox is good; nevertheless, if it leads us to think that by it alone we are going to heaven, we are deceived. **'Even the demons believe that — and shudder.'** The demons have that kind of faith, but it falls short of saving faith. There is not a single atheist, polytheist, pantheist or agnostic among all the demonic host. To be sure, we must begin with intellectual assent and agreement; however, there must be that third and vital element of faith — *trust*.

## The example of Abraham's faith (2:20-24)

James rebukes those who regard works as an unnecessary add-on to faith: **'You foolish man '** (2:20). He then proceeds to prove that **'faith without deeds is useless'**, using the example of Abraham to show a correct relationship between faith and works. Three features of his life are mentioned.

### 1. His qualifications (2:21,23)

Abraham is described as 'our father' (RSV, compare with **'ancestor'** in the NIV). This description (cf. Isa. 51:2) would have carried great weight for Jewish readers, who looked back to him as the founder of the nation of Israel. James, however, writes as a Christian. The New Testament views Abraham as the father of all who believe (Rom. 4:11). Believers in Christ, whether Jew or Gentile, can look back to Abraham as the father of their faith.

He is also called **'God's friend'** (cf. 2 Chr. 20:7; Isa. 41:8). The hallmark of friendship is that two parties get on well. Faith is set forth as the means of removing enmity with God and finding peace and reconciliation with him.

Abraham's qualifications connect him to us (as our father) and to God (as friend). Taken together, these horizontal and vertical dimensions make him the measure and model of faith for every man and woman.

### 2. His test (2:21)

In Scripture, Abraham is set forth as the great exemplar of faith (Gen. 11 – 25; Rom. 4; Gal. 3; Heb. 11). It was his faith that led him from his own country to the land God promised to him and his descendants (Gen. 12:1-3; Acts 7:2-8). He became a pilgrim by faith and in the promised land of Canaan God made a covenant with him (Gen. 15). God attached promises to that covenant regarding Abraham's future. Those promises had their focus in a son. After years of waiting, Isaac was eventually born to Abraham in his old age when his wife Sarah had ceased to be able to bear children by normal biological processes.

Abraham faced many tests of his faith during his life, but James selects just one. He recalls the day on which Abraham was commanded by God to sacrifice the miraculous son of his old age, Isaac (Gen. 22). If Isaac was killed the covenant would be finished and his future hopes dashed. Yet Abraham did what God commanded even though he did not under-stand. As he lifted the knife to slay his son, God intervened and said, 'Do not lay a hand on the boy… Now I know that you fear God' (Gen. 22:12). God's command to Abraham was a test of his faith (Gen. 22:1, cf. James 1:3). But from a different perspective this could also be said to be Abraham's greatest deed, the climax of his walk of faith.

### 3. His maturity (2:22)

How are we to explain Abraham's painful act of obedience? Where did he find the strength to rise above natural emo-tions? James explains it in terms of Abraham's faith and refers to a Bible verse (**'And the Scripture was fulfilled that says …'**) which was fulfilled, not in the prophetic sense, but rather in that it concurs with James' explanation (Gen. 15:6). He quotes the very same verse that Paul draws on more than once to explain that we are justified by faith *apart from works* (Rom. 4:3,9,22; Gal. 3:6). Abraham's *faith* was the principle behind all that he did and the secret of his friendship with God.

Genesis 15:6 establishes *the primacy of faith* in order to please God and to rightly relate to him. This is the point that Paul brings out so often in his letters. James, on the other hand, points back to the same verse to stress not so much the primacy of faith as *faith as the source of Abraham's obedience* in offering Isaac, an action that completed and confirmed the validity of that faith shown years ago when **'Abraham believed God'**. In this sense James can say that **'... a person is justified by what he does and not by faith alone.'**

James was as conversant with the Scriptures as Paul was. He knew that Abraham was accounted righteous well before he offered Isaac. The act of obedience in offering Isaac confirmed his faith in God as genuine. The point is that faith is never alone. It always shows itself in works, and not just any works, but works of obedience. When we ask how many, or what kind of, works we need to be saved, the answer is 'None'. Only Christ's work gets us to heaven. The question is not *how many* works, but *whether our faith is real*, as evidenced by our works, imperfect as they are (see the further discussion on this topic in the section headed 'The interpretation of James 2:24').

Notice that James describes Abraham as a man whose 'faith was made perfect' by works (2:22, RSV). The same idea of perfection that was introduced at the beginning of the letter reappears (cf. 'perfect and complete', 1:4, RSV). Here is a further link to what we have seen to be the central theme of this letter, which is maturity reached through trials while we wait patiently for the Lord to return.

**The example of Rahab's faith** (2:25)

Abraham's faith was tested throughout his life. By comparison Rahab is known for only one work of faith. The description **'Rahab the prostitute'** is shocking, especially as she is offered as an example of vital faith. Perhaps that is why James adds the identifying label, 'the prostitute'. Here is a woman of ill repute with a permanent reminder of her past added to her name. Yet our past does not matter when faith brings new life.

> Pardon for sin and a peace that endureth,
> Thine own dear presence to cheer and to guide;
> Strength for today and bright hope for tomorrow…

is the glorious lot of every man or woman of faith. No one can take these privileges away from the child of God, no matter how shameful our past life may have been. Paul could likewise rejoice in the grace of Christ though formerly he was 'a blasphemer and a persecutor and a violent man' (1 Tim. 1:13).

But this is surely not the primary reason that Rahab is mentioned here. Nor is it the contrast between her and Abraham, startling though that is. Abraham was a spiritual giant in redemptive history, the founding father of God's covenant people, a man with a respected status in society and one who displayed trust in God over many years. Rahab is no such person. Indeed, she is just the opposite, yet she enjoys the same blessing as Abraham. What a bold reminder of how precious and all-encompassing faith is! Eternal life is promised to all who *believe*, so that in the economy of the kingdom of God natural advantages such as race, gender, status, or other privileges, count for nothing. However, placing Rahab alongside Abraham, as James does, goes only so far in explaining her presence in the text.

The story of Rahab is found in the book of Joshua (Josh. 2:1-24; 6:22-25). Her one recorded act of faith in receiving the spies finds its way into the letter of James at this point because it goes beyond a sentimental or intellectual faith. She did not merely say to the spies, 'Go, I wish you well; keep warm and well fed' (2:16). She warmed and filled them, concealing them under the stalks of flax on the roof, and convinced the city authorities that the spies had left by another way. She could indeed say, 'I wish you well,' because by her actions she had in effect saved their lives.

Her faith was more than knowledge and agreement (2:18). She had heard 'how the LORD dried up the water of the Red Sea' (Josh. 2:10) and how the two kings of the Amorites had been destroyed. She acknowledged to the spies that these were no ordinary acts of human strength, 'for the LORD your God is God in heaven above and on earth below' (Josh. 2:11). She believed in the coming judgement of God that would destroy her own city. All of this is commendable, but it was Rahab's costly act of identification with the God of Israel and his people that demonstrated her vital saving faith: **'… she gave lodging to the spies and sent them off in a different direction'** — a deed that, if discovered, would have resulted in her death as a traitor. Rahab provides further proof that works naturally follow faith and are the necessary verification of it.

## Conclusion and application (2:26)

James returns in verse 26 to his initial premise that faith without works is dead (cf. 2:17,20). The point is made by way of analogy: **'As the body without the spirit is dead, so faith without deeds is dead.'** The word **'spirit'** could also be translated as 'breath', in which case James is making an observation from the world of nature, as he does elsewhere. Otherwise he is drawing from biblical anthropology in which at creation man becomes 'a living being', consisting of both body and spirit when the Lord breathed into him the breath of life (Gen. 2:7). The point remains the same whichever way it is translated. Faith separate from works is like a body without its breath of life, which, wonderful though it may appear, is dead and subject to decay.

James repeats his assertion that **'faith without deeds'** is dead (2:26; cf. 2:17). Again he never mentions 'deeds without faith', because it would be unthinkable to him that works can ever bring us into a right standing with God. This would be a denial of salvation by God's grace. If our deeds could contribute even the smallest amount to our salvation, then man is not cut off from God, the apostolic witness is false and the Scripture is untrue when it claims that 'All have sinned and fall short of the glory of God' (Rom. 3:23). Only God could rescue us. Only on the foundation of the cross, which alone satisfies the righteous requirements of a holy God, are we justified. Only by the instrumentality of faith is the 'alien righteousness' of God reckoned to us, as James clearly indicates (2:23). James is not talking down faith here, any more than he is talking up works. He is concerned that we grasp the proper connection between the two.

The disconnection of works from faith weaves its way like a trail of breadcrumbs through church history. Charles Spurgeon preached against this error which he observed in the church of own day:

> It has been supposed by many ill-instructed people that the doctrine of justification by faith is opposed to the teaching of good works or obedience. There is no truth in the supposition. We preach the obedience of faith. Faith is the fountain, the foundation and the foster of obedience. Men obey not God until they believe in him. We preach faith in order that men may be brought to obedience. To disbelieve is to disobey…
>
> I remember a place in Yorkshire, years ago, where a good man said to me, 'We have a real good minister.' I said, 'I am glad to hear it.' 'Yea,' he said; 'he is a fellow that preaches with his feet.' Well, now, that is a capital thing if a preacher preaches with his feet by walking with God, and with his hands by working for

God. He does well who glorifies God by where he goes, and by what he does; he will excel fifty others who only preach religion with their tongues. You, dear hearers, are not good hearers so long as you are only hearers; but when the heart is affected by the ear, and the hand follows the heart, then your faith is proved. That kind of obedience which comes of faith in God is real obedience, since it shows itself by its works.[1]

More recently, Dietrich Bonhoeffer coined the phrase 'cheap grace' to describe the type of faith that does not produce a change of life. He writes, 'Cheap grace is the preaching of forgiveness without requiring repentance, baptism without church discipline, Communion without confession, absolution without personal confession. Cheap grace is grace without discipleship, grace without the cross, grace without Jesus Christ, living and incarnate.'[2] This form of 'easy-believism' wants Christ without the cost and is another manifestation of faith without works.

## The interpretation of James 2:24

One commentator calls verse 24 of chapter 2 'a *crux inter-pretum*, not only for James, but for NT theology in general.'[3] Interpretations other than the one suggested above abound, some of which read verse 24 as a full-frontal attack on the Pauline doctrine of justification by faith alone. Indeed, it is this verse more than any other that has brought tension over the place of James in the canon of Scripture. Several factors combine to heighten that tension. James and Paul are addressing the same topic — namely, the place of works in justification; each one appeals to Abraham as an illustration (James 2:21-24; Rom. 4:1-25); they quote the same passage in Genesis 15:6 in support (James 2:23; Rom. 4:3); they use similar items of vocabulary (faith, works, justify); and both are polemical. Yet apparently different conclusions are reached by way of strikingly similar statements (but oppositely worded):

'A man is justified by works and not by faith alone' (James 2:24, RSV)

'A man is justified by faith apart from works of law' (Rom. 3:28, RSV)

So, while James and Paul argue that faith is essential to justification, they may appear to take contrary positions on the role of works. James seems to say that we can help ourselves by adding works of obedience to the grace of God in order to obtain salvation. Paul denies any such role for our works in justification.

Many lines of enquiry have been pursued in an effort to resolve this conflict:

1. Is there *a difference in the kind of works being described*? Is Paul thinking of works of the law (e.g. Rom. 9:32; Gal. 3:10) whereas James is dealing with works of love (2:15-17)? In the final analysis they come to much the same thing. The issue is not about the *nature* of the works but their *role* in justification.

2. Another approach is to *modify Paul to agree with James*. Justification, it is suggested, can be thought of as a process that takes place throughout the believer's life and which is finally decided at the last judgement. One is justified at first by faith alone, but then later by works in addition to faith. The result is two justifications: an initial admission into a right standing with God, followed by a final vindication in the judgement. This approach goes strongly against Paul's own strong insistence that grace alone through faith secures in the present that future final verdict from a just and holy God. Further, it undermines any assurance of salvation. On this view Paul could never have written, 'Therefore, there is now no condemnation for those who are in Christ Jesus' (Rom. 8:1), because justification would never be final until a person was finally justified.

3. Alternatively, Paul's teaching can be modified by taking justification right out of the category of salvation and making it *a church membership issue*, which is proposed by the so-called New Perspective movement on Paul. Suffice it to say that the New Perspective is a serious misreading of Paul.[4]

4. A more productive approach has been to recognize that *James and Paul address two different audiences* and two understandings of faith. Paul is engaged in Gentile mission and writes polemically against Judaizers who insist on the circumcision of Gentile converts. He considers the act of

circumcision to be a work of the law added to faith. For Paul, faith is trust in the promises of God fulfilled by Christ and so he refers to the initial response of Abraham, who *believed* God and it was reckoned to him as righteousness (Gen. 15:6) long before he was circumcised.

Is Paul unconcerned about the place of works in the Christian life? Not at all. Paul places the importance of good works alongside teaching that justification is by grace through faith alone (Eph. 2:8-10; Titus 3:5-8). Paul can write, 'He saved us, *not because of the righteous things we had done*, but because of his mercy.' After which he continues: 'I want you to stress these things, so that those who have trusted in God may be careful to *devote themselves to doing what is good*' (Titus 3:5,8, italics added).

By contrast, James is admonishing Christian Jews, some of whom thought that works were unimportant, so that their so-called 'faith' failed to affect their conduct. James writes forcefully against this sterile faith which was devoid of genuine compassion. It believes certain truths about God, but is really no faith at all. So when James appeals to Abraham for support he points to a subsequent action (Gen. 22) which arose out of his initial faith (Gen. 15:6) and makes the point that Abraham *obeyed* God (2:22). The faith that Paul commends is clearly not the same as that which James condemns.

5. Finally, *consideration needs to be given to the verb* translated as **'considered righteous'** in verse 21 (Greek, *dikaioō*). We might note that it is differently translated as **'is justified'** in verse 24. Yet, in the following verse, 2:25, we revert back to **'considered righteous'**. The two look different but in fact derive from the same word.[5]

Most words have a range of meanings; which one is intended must be finally determined by the context. Paul, for example, uses 'to justify' (*dikaioō*) to refer to that initial and judicial action of God's free grace in which the sinner who trusts in Christ is fully pardoned, declared 'not guilty' and acquitted, and accepted as righteous only for the righteousness of Christ imputed to him or her. Those with a Reformation heritage naturally read Paul's use into James. Yet that is not necessarily fair to James, since he was probably writing before Paul and, as has been argued above, within a different framework of reference.

James draws much of his thinking from the teachings of Jesus found in Matthew's Gospel, as well as from the Old Testament, and writes at a time when the infant church was just emerging out of Judaism.

There are two possible understandings of *dikaioō* that need to be considered when reading the letter of James.

### The declarative sense

In the Greek Old Testament (called the Septuagint) *dikaioō* can mean 'to declare righteous' or 'to vindicate in the judgement'. The declarative meaning is found in many passages with a legal setting (Deut. 25:1; Prov. 17:15) and sometimes, significantly, with God as Judge (Exod. 23:7; 1 Kings 8:32; Micah 6:11). In the parable of the Pharisee and the tax collector, the tax collector went down to his house having been declared righteous (Luke 18:14). Matthew's Gospel uses this definition when Jesus says, 'For by your words you will be justified and by your words you will be condemned' (Matt. 12:37, RSV). It is important in Paul's letters as well (Rom. 8:33-34).

If this is the sense James intends, then he is saying that in the final judgement God will take into account a person's works as evidence of the genuineness of his or her faith. These works come from the 'good life' of believers and are equivalent to what James describes as 'deeds done in the humility that comes from wisdom' (3:13). The *Westminster Confession* describes the status of these works in the following way:

We cannot by our best works merit pardon of sin, or eternal life at the hand of God, by reason of the great disproportion that is between them and the glory to come; and the infinite distance that is between us and God, whom, by them, we can neither profit, nor satisfy for the debt of our former sins, but when we have done all we can, we have done but our duty, and are unprofitable servants: and because, as they are good, they proceed from His Spirit, and as they are wrought by us, they are defiled, and mixed with so much weakness and imperfection, that they cannot endure the severity of God's judgement.[6]

## The demonstrative sense

In the Septuagint the verb *dikaioō* can also mean 'to show to be righteous' (see Job 32:2). In the New Testament a lawyer wanted 'to justify' himself, asking, 'Who is my neighbour?' (Luke 10:29). Jesus taught that 'Wisdom *is proved right* by her actions' (Matt. 11:19, italics mine), in the sense of demonstrating something to be right by one's deeds. Corrupt human wisdom produces corrupt human actions; divine wisdom, taught by Jesus and John, produces right actions resulting in obedient lives. The demonstrative reading of *dikaioō* for the letter of James is appealing because, if adopted, it can be far more easily reconciled with Paul's teaching. James is saying that Abraham is 'shown to be righteous' by his works, and not simply by his faith.

Since either the declarative or the demonstrative sense can be adopted without affecting the overall interpretation proposed, the choice between them is not as critical as sometimes suggested.

# 14.
# Teachers of the Word

*Please read James 3:1-5*

Human language is a wonderful gift. It is the primary way by which we communicate with one another. Learning to speak is one of the first and longest educational processes — an indicator of the complexity of language learning. We begin to speak our first words at about the age of twelve months. We start with single words like 'Mummy' and, of course, that word feared by all parents, 'No!' By the time we are eighteen months old our vocabulary has grown to fifty words, by the age of three years to a thousand words, and by that time we are adding at least two words a day. Then we learn the process of joining words together with the complex rules and conventions of our own mother tongue. In 1950 *Webster's Dictionary* contained about 400.000 words. Today that number has nearly doubled. New words are being invented all the time — words like 'slam dunk', 'compact disc' and 'mobile phone'.

But have we thought about the power of words? Words communicate our thoughts, ideas, motives, hopes and dreams. They reveal our feelings — we love and hate with our words. Wars are started by words, yet 'a gentle answer turns away wrath' (Prov. 15:1). So many deep and varied feelings are stirred and conveyed simply through verbal communication. It is amazing how speech is used not just to share our innermost selves, but also to influence entire communities. History has witnessed some powerful addresses that have gripped and inspired whole nations. Think of the following examples:

> And so my fellow Americans, ask not what your country can do for you; ask what you can do for your country (John Kennedy).

> I have a dream that one day this nation will rise up and live out the true meaning of this creed: that all men are created equal (Martin Luther King on racial equality).

> But if the British Empire and its Commonwealth last for a thousand years men will still say, 'This was their finest hour' (Winston Spencer Churchill on the Battle of Britain).

The Bible is called 'the Word of God', which is a reminder that God chose words to communicate with us. Indeed he sent his Son, Jesus Christ, the incarnate and personal Word, to speak his final word and to secure our salvation by the blood of the eternal covenant. God's Word is an abiding power (Isa. 40:8); it is the power for salvation to all who believe (Rom. 1:16), and we are called to live by it each day (Matt. 4:4). And, because we are created in God's image and likeness, our words have power too, albeit temporal and limited. They have the potential for good and (because of sin) evil.

The main idea of this section is how words, small though they are, have a massive influence on our lives, both individually and corporately. James begins with a caution to aspiring teachers, whose stock-in-trade is words (3:1), widens it to include every man and woman (3:2) and, using 'the tongue' as a metonym for speech, closes with an illustration which leads into the next section (3:5).

The striking feature of verses 1-5 is the pairs of contrasts. A distinction is made between something substantial, or powerful, on the one hand, and something small and apparently of little significance, on the other. The following table sets out this literary structure:

| *Verse* | *Great* | *Small* |
| --- | --- | --- |
| 3:1 | The greater judgement of teachers | (No contrast offered) |
| 3:2 | The whole body of a person (all of a person's activities) | A person's words |
| 3:3 | The powerful body of a horse | Turned by a bit placed in the mouth |
| 3:4 | Large ships driven by strong winds | Small rudder |
| 3:4 | Large ships | The pilot who steers the ship |
| 3:5 | Great boasts (great plans and achievements) | The tongue — a small part of the body |
| 3:5 | The great forest fire | A small spark |

It is interesting that the writer offers no contrast with regard to future judgement (3:1). It is as if the judgement of God is so exacting, and of such a different order, that nothing can be contrasted with it. It is a sobering reminder that God will bring to account everything in our lives. For those who hanker to be teachers of the church this has huge entailments — but more of that later.

It is difficult to know where to make divisions in this section of James. The NIV chooses to make a break after verse 6, the RSV after verse 5, whereas the UBS Greek text makes the break halfway through verse 5. The reason for this is that verse 5 is transitional. Verses 1-5 establish the power of words to regulate life, using illustrations which are generally positive. The section which follows (3:6-12) shows the corrupting nature of the tongue, using largely negative references. But the **'great boasts'** of verse 5 are capable of interpretation either positively or negatively. Undeniably, the tongue has the talent to advertise great plans and accomplishments, some of which may be evil and an indicator of pride (4:16) but not necessarily so (3:9). The subsequent illustration in the second part of verse 5 of the spark causing the great forest fire, however, prepares the reader for the injurious evil that the tongue can and does commit.

## All (especially teachers) are responsible for their words (3:1-2)

The table on the previous page indicates that James is not yet describing the way the tongue tarnishes our life (that comes later, in 3:6-12); rather, he draws attention to the influence the teacher exercises within the church. A bricklayer lays bricks; a pharmacist dispenses drugs; and a teacher speaks words. Words are the primary tool by which the teacher carries out his work. It may not be the case that a teacher speaks more than anyone else, but his words reach more people and carry greater weight.

The introduction of the appointment of teachers into the text at this point seems out of place, yet it is there for several reasons. The previous section looks at the relationship between faith and works. The question must be asked, 'What kind of works is James thinking of?' What should we look for as evidence of a living faith? The answer lies (though not exclusively) in the words which we speak. Speech is not a new topic, as it has been mentioned several times before, and will be again, before the end of the letter (cf. 1:19-20; 2:12-16; 3:1-12; 4:11-15; 5:9-12). However, as the opening of the letter suggests, James is writing to churches (1:1). The health and well-being of the church of Jesus Christ are very much on James' mind. The teacher in these Jewish Christian churches would have been regarded in much the same way as a rabbi, a respected and highly valued profession in Jewish society (John 1:38). So James knows that the one who teaches God's people (and he includes himself — **'we who teach'**) has a major influence in the church.

To teach the Word is to invite close and particular scrutiny from God. It is to venture into an area of ministry where influence is great, temptations are strong and sins are easily committed, and none should enter it lightly. Hence a caution is given to those who eagerly and thoughtlessly desired a role which carried considerable prestige in the early church.

The work of the teacher is to teach the Word of God. The Word is the final authority in all matters of faith and practice. The teacher has no other brief than to faithfully explain and apply its teachings. He is not at liberty to engage in overly speculative discussion, nor is he to teach his own ideas and opinions. Even so, he has to use his own words to convey the great truths contained in Scripture. And when God's Word is preached, the Holy Spirit breathes life into it and it goes forth in power and authority, challenging and convicting men and women of its saving truths, and laying bare the thoughts and intentions of the heart (Heb. 4:12).

Although the teacher has a wonderful ministry, James warns, 'Don't rush into it!' Teachers will be judged with greater strictness, because of the disproportionate influence they exert. He is thinking of the future Day of Judgement and warning not just that 'every careless word' (Matt. 12:36) will be called to account, but that teachers face a much more exacting standard of judgement. We are reminded of the dreadful woes that Jesus pronounced on teachers of the law in his day who failed to practise what they taught (Matt. 23:13-29). It is all too easy to lead people astray by teaching something that is not true, that is unbalanced or misleading. Paul says to Timothy, 'Watch your life and doctrine closely. Persevere in them, because if you do, you will save both yourself and your hearers' (1 Tim. 4:16).

The thought of judgement is broadened in verse 2 to include not just teachers, but every individual. The NIV version omits to translate the conjunction 'for' which connects verse 2 to verse 1 (literally it reads: 'for we all stumble in many ways'). An additional reason for the admonition to would-be teachers is that they engage in an activity in which we all stumble and which is more susceptible to sin than others — namely, speaking. The fact that James uses the word **'we'** may refer to mankind in general — a reference to the fallen nature of man. If so, he is making a general statement to the effect that our words get all of us into trouble at one time or another.

When James says, **'If anyone is never at fault in what he says, he is a perfect man'**, he is not suggesting that freedom from sins of speech is an attainable condition. Though there may be some sins that we have never committed, we are all united in having committed this one, the sin of speech. Notice again how James picks up the main theme of the letter — the quest for Christian maturity. He applies the same word translated as 'mature' (1:4) to the man who is able to control his words, describing him as **'a perfect man'** (Greek, *teleios*). Careful supervision of the tongue is an infallible index of spiritual health and maturity.

James adds that the perfect man is **'able to keep his whole body in check'**. Some commentators, noting James' frequent use of the word **'body'** in this section, want to make a link with the 'body' of Christ — the church. This connection seems all the more attractive given the mention of teachers in the church. But it is doubtful whether such a connection was in the mind of James. The body metaphor of the church is found and developed in Paul's letters, but nowhere else. James uses the word only to describe the physical torso of the horse (translated 'animal' in 3:3), or human being (3:6), or in this case, as a figure of speech standing for the idea of the complete man (3:2).

## The disproportionate power of speech (3:3-4)

James highlights the exceptional power of words by referring to examples from life. The first picture is that of horses. They were the chief means of rapid transport and communication, but they needed to be broken in order to be controlled. In the wild they are strong, impetuous animals, but place a piece of metal called a 'bit' in a horse's mouth and attach it to the reins, and even a child can be in command of the horse. The bit gives us complete control and **'we can turn the whole animal'**.

The second illustration — **'Or take ships as an example'** — is of sailing vessels. These were the largest known man-made means of transport and trade. Some of the first-century vessels were over sixty metres (nearly 200 feet) long and twenty metres (sixty-five feet) wide. A Roman merchant ship could carry an enormous cargo (around 300 to 400 metric tonnes) and harness the wind to move quickly through the ocean. Yet the pilot, by means of a tiny rudder (in comparison to the size of the ship), manoeuvres and sends that ship in whatever direction he wants it to go. It is an apt illustration that something so small can be so controlling.

Words likewise have mighty power. Mary Queen of Scots said she was more afraid of the preaching of John Knox than she was of 10,000 soldiers. Think of how the word of the gospel has influenced millions of individual lives, and even whole civilizations.


## The impact of the tongue (3:5)

As James comes to apply the above illustrations, with the words, **'Likewise the tongue is a …'**, he begins to hint at the potential of our words for evil, thus setting the scene for further development in the following section by giving us two word pictures (3:6-12).

The first is the capacity of this **'small part of the body'** to boast. Whether boasting is justified or not depends upon the context and what is boasted. Given what follows, however, we should conceive it to be largely misplaced boasting. Though small in size, weighing perhaps only 100 grams (or 3½ ounces), the little piece of red flesh wedged into the mouth can make extravagant and arrogant claims (see, for example 4:13). We need only recall some of the famous athletes in the past who publicly paraded their athletic prowess. In media interviews they managed an uncanny flair for self-promotion and yet today they are in many cases largely forgotten. The psalmist likens the tongue to a sharpened razor (Ps. 52:2). Think of the arrogant boasters of Scripture, beginning with Lamech (Gen. 4:23-24). Not that the tongue itself is the real problem; it is the sinful human heart that stands behind it.

The second illustration, also transitional, is most definitely negative: **'Consider what a great forest is set on fire…'** In Australia the heat of summer turns the landscape brown, and the grass in the paddock becomes so dry it crumbles beneath the feet. Out in the bush — those huge tracts of eucalyptus forest — 'the Big Dry' brings the threat of bush fire. Local shire councils erect signs at the side of the road to indicate the degree of fire danger, and people who live in the bush are encouraged to make adequate preparation to defend their properties should fires strike. And strike they do, sometimes with little warning and terrifying speed, destroying all in their path. James encourages us to ponder the fact that this destructive force can be started **'by a small spark'** — a car exhaust, a carelessly discarded cigarette butt or a glass bottle.

An athlete friend in Victoria rang his brother, in Queensland, some 2,000 kilometres (over 1,200 miles) away, to ask whether a rumour of a national coach using performance-enhancing drugs was true. Within hours the sports reporter of a major newspaper rang to get comment on this 'hot' story. A rumour once started cannot be stopped. My friend confessed he had never thought such an innocent and private enquiry could take wings and fly so quickly. That is the property of words — little things in themselves, yet powerful and sometimes deadly. One careless word, one thoughtless remark, one angry response, one vindictive reply, one defamatory comment, and a whole world of relationships is set ablaze and incalculable damage inflicted. Words have a profound potential for good, but the reverse is sadly (and more commonly) the case.


## Conclusion

We have seen that the warnings on the power of speech are initially directed to those desiring to become teachers in the church, even though James broadens his appeals in subsequent verses. Hence, we should not lose sight of the truth that teachers of the Word of God have a critical role in the health of the church. They can lead God's people to maturity, or into spiritual decline and disunity. While it is the case that we all stumble in many ways (3:2), the stumbling teacher trips up not only himself, but those whom he teaches.

From what James has written so far, we may infer that the maturity of God's people (1:4) is dependent on both the manner in which they listen to God's Word (1:19-25) and on the quality of Christian teachers that are appointed to speak in the church (3:1-5). John Stott, addressing teachers and preachers towards the end of the twentieth century, sounds the same cautionary note as James:

Today's preachers are neither prophets nor apostles, for we are not the recipients of any fresh, direct revelation. The Word of the Lord does not come to us as it came to them; rather we have come to it. Nevertheless, if we faithfully expound the Scriptures, it is his Word which is in our hands and on our lips, and the Holy Spirit is able to make it into a living and powerful word in the hearts of our hearers. Moreover, our responsibility will appear to us the more onerous when we remember the indissoluble link which we have traced between the Word of God and the people of God. A deaf church is a dead church: that is an unalterable principle. God quickens, feeds, inspires and guides his people by his Word. For whenever the Bible is truly and systematically expounded, God uses it to give his people the vision without which they perish. First, they begin to see what he wants them to be, his new society in the world. Then they go on to grasp the resources he has given to them in Christ to fulfil his purpose. That is why it is only by humble and obedient listening to his voice that the Church can grow into maturity, serve the world and glorify its Lord.[1]

# 15.
# The tongue of fire

*Please read James 3:6-12*

If the last section was about the power of words, this one is about the misuse of words. Some of the greatest evils in human history have come about through words. In the Garden of Eden the words of the serpent raised doubts in the mind of Eve about the command of God and, indeed, his goodness. Cain's treacherous words to Abel were followed by murderous actions (Gen. 4:8). Lamech's words were vindictive and cruel (Gen. 4:23-24). The generation following the Flood used their common language to unite in pride against God by trying to build a tower up to heaven (Gen. 11). Only God's gracious confusion of their speech limited man's rebellion. Indeed, were it not for God's restraining grace on our words, society would quickly fall into chaos and ruin.

Cautionary teaching on the use of the tongue is one of the characteristics of Jewish Wisdom literature. A quick sampling of the book of Proverbs reveals concerns with the double-edged nature of our words (Prov. 12:18; 15:1,4), their insufficiency unless accompanied by actions (Prov. 14:23), the importance of listening carefully before speaking (Prov. 18:13) and the need not just to speak the truth, but to speak out for the weak and vulnerable (Prov. 14:25; 31:8-9). James focuses on the destructive potential of the tongue and our need of grace.


**The unrighteous tongue** (3:6)

God made the tongue. Like all that God made, he made it good (Gen. 1:31); it is not intrinsically evil. The tongue is, of course, not the real cause of evil; it does not operate as an independent member of the body. The real cause of wickedness is the heart — the governing centre of our personality — which is fallen and biased towards evil. The word **'tongue'**, as James uses it, then, stands for our words, and lying behind our words is the heart.

James moves from simile (the tongue is *like* a bit, a rudder, a spark) to metaphor: **'The tongue … *is* a fire'** (italics added). The tongue, says James, is **'a world of evil'** — the essence of all in life that is fallen and hostile to God. This is then followed, in the second part of verse 6, by three parallel clauses which explain the effect, extent and source of the tongue's evil.

While we were working as missionaries in West Java one of the local volcanoes erupted, spewing out molten rock. Even though the volcano was 100 kilometres (over sixty miles) away, the prevailing winds brought thick clouds of volcanic ash drifting over the landscape for several days. Visibility was reduced to a few metres, on top of which we were forced to wear handkerchiefs over our mouths to stop ourselves choking and to switch on the headlights of the car in the middle of the day in order to see the road ahead. The grey ash was light and powdery, seeping into every nook and cranny and settling to a depth of several centimetres. It was impossible to keep anything clean. The house, our hair, our clothes, our belongings, and even our food, were all contaminated. It is a picture of the effect that the evil of the tongue has on our whole being. It **'corrupts the whole person'** — shaping our thinking, damaging our emotional stability, warping our desires and affecting the physical members of the body as we turn our words into actions.

Words influence our actions. Words build psychological connections, creating impressions and expectations. In fact language is one of the principal means for forming and controlling human conduct. Words not only express ideas, but direct behaviour. So the words of Jesus, 'I have compassion for these people', led to an act of compassion in feeding those who were hungry (Matt. 15:32-38). On the other hand, angry words can lead to angry behaviour which may involve other members of the body, such as the fists. Management of our speech puts us in the enviable position of ascendancy over the whole person. If we can master the tongue, the most unmanageable part of our anatomy, then we can master every other faculty of the body where discipline or restraint is needed.

James not only tells us of the defiling effect of the tongue, but of the extent of its influence on our life. The tongue **'sets the whole course of his life on fire'**. This second clause reverts back to the fire metaphor, translating a difficult phrase (meaning the 'wheel of existence') as 'the whole course of life'. Some of the sins we enjoyed when we were young we can no longer commit later on because of the incapacity of old age. The sins of the tongue, however, are just as vigorous and strong in old age as they were in youth — indeed, perhaps more so. A visit to a home for the elderly can be revealing. The mind weakened by age no longer has the capacity to conceal what it once could. What had been restrained through education and superficial politeness rises to the surface and the results are sometimes unpleasant.

Then the third clause adds, **'and is itself set on fire by hell'**, meaning that the source of the tongue's power can be traced back to, literally, 'Gehenna'. I recently walked through Gehenna. Today it is a pleasant green valley just south of the city walls of Jerusalem, but in biblical times Gehenna was the city rubbish dump. It was always burning. The corpses of executed criminals were buried there, together with all the city's garbage and sewage. In the Bible it came to be used as an image of hell. Elsewhere Scripture gives examples of how the chief inhabitant of hell — Satan himself — can use our words. He is the unseen driver behind the tongue's malevolent potency. When Ananias lied to the church about the property he sold, Peter asked him, 'Ananias, how is it that Satan has so filled your heart that you have lied to the Holy Spirit?' (Acts 5:3). Where did this falsehood come from? It came from Satan himself as he tried to corrupt the fellowship of the early church. Satan gets into our lives through our words more than through any other avenue.

The sins of the tongue are not even restricted to lying or bad language. The apostle Peter gave Jesus what he thought was good advice and tried to turn him from the Father's will, the sufferings of the cross. Jesus rebuked him and said, 'Get behind me, Satan! … You do not have in mind the things of God, but the things of men' (Mark 8:33). Even well-meaning advice, uncontrolled by the Word and Spirit of God, can be from hell itself. Are we not ashamed when we review our lives and failure at this point? We need the Saviour's forgiveness and his wisdom to learn to speak as he did — words of grace and truth.

**The untameable tongue** (3:7-8)

James, the keen observer of life, draws an analogy between the world of nature and our spiritual life. The four divisions of living things in verse 7 reflect the pattern of creation in Genesis 1:28. Integral to God's plan is that man is not alone in his creation, but is part of a hierarchy of nature over which he is given the mandate to rule and to subdue it. It is to this chain of command that James appeals. Despite his sinfulness man has learnt to domesticate or tame just about every living creature. What a wonderful picture of the glory of man as steward and vicegerent of God's world!

**'But'**, says James, **'no man can tame the tongue'** (3:8). The contrast is razor-sharp. Man's glory is set alongside his shame. Listen to the way we speak to each other and about each other. Observe the effect the tongue has on relationships, behaviour and attitudes. The tongue remains unwavering and defiant of every attempt to tame it. It is full of deadly poison, injuring and killing. Divisions among God's redeemed people are caused and exacerbated by the misuse of the tongue. This is to our shame and a hindrance to evangelism because it makes it difficult for people to believe in the gospel's life-changing power.

**The inconsistent tongue** (3:9-10)

'Oh, for a thousand tongues …!', we sing with gusto. The thousand tongues we use to bless **'our Lord and Father'** (and, yes, that is good) can also be used to **'curse men, who have been made in God's likeness'**. Notice that men retain the likeness of God despite the spoiling effects of sin (Gen. 1:27). In the beginning God made man in his own image to reflect the perfections of the divine nature. This distinguished man from the rest of the created order of **'animals, birds, reptiles and creatures of the sea'** (3:7), conferring upon him dignity and respect. Hence to inflict an injury on man is tantamount to an attack on God himself (Gen. 9:6). Similarly, the call to be consistent in the use of our tongues has to do with God, whose image still resides in man. Again theology undergirds ethical imperatives.

The issue of double-mindedness raised in connection with prayer (1:5-8) surfaces here in relation to speech. The same tongue used to bless God is employed to curse man. John Blanchard, writing on this passage, powerfully applies it to what can happen immediately following a service of worship:

A friend once told me that one of the most challenging sermons he had ever heard was called 'Ten minutes after the benediction'. It spoke of those who moved in moments from the gloria to gossip, from creed to criticism, from worshipping God to wounding men. Can we plead 'not guilty' to that sort of thing? That is the kind of inconsistency James is attacking and it is little wonder that he adds, 'My brothers, this should not be.' The thing is not only inconsistent, it is iniquitous.

Has James overdone it in taking up so much space in warning us about the use of the tongue? Surely not. No sensitive Christian ought to be able to read his words without a sense of shame, mingled with the longing to know in his own life God's answer to the psalmist's prayer:

May the words of my mouth and the meditation of my
    heart
be pleasing in your sight,
O LORD, my Rock and my Redeemer

(Ps. 19:14).[1]

**Lessons from nature** (3:11-12)

All of this is very disheartening and mostly negative. None of us escapes the force of James' teaching. When it comes to the tongue, we all suffer from galloping halitosis (i.e. bad breath!). The words we say to one another (or more often *of* one another) are sometimes so 'heated' they can peel the paint off the wall. Should we then abandon the quest for self-control and Christian maturity (1:4) at this point? Is it really possible for the man or woman of faith to show evidence of maturity (2:14-17) by controlled speech? Is there any hope offered in these verses? I believe there is.

As he applies the teaching of the previous verses to his readers, James asks some important questions. Reverting to type as an astute observer of the environment, he says it is impossible to find certain things in nature. You cannot find a spring that produces both **'fresh water and salt water'**. A **'fig tree'** never grows **'olives'**. You can never harvest **'figs'** from a **'grapevine'**. What does he mean?

I believe James is saying that our words reveal the state of our hearts more than does any other measure of spirituality. Our Lord Jesus taught, 'Out of the overflow of the heart the mouth speaks' (Matt. 12:34). You can draw a straight line from the tongue (which is seen) to the heart (which is not). Our words betray where we stand spiritually. Bitter words expose a heart that is bitter, angry words an angry heart, boastful words a proud heart, and so on.

Paradoxically this also reveals the solution. If the core problem is the heart, then change has to begin there. We must not run away from this. If God has shown us our sin here, then we must look to him for pardon and strength to change. He alone can renew the heart. Even if we have been Christians for many years, the answer is to go back to the gospel remedy, back to him, and seek his pardon and grace to change. And we need to keep on going back. Repentance is not a single act, but a habit to learn. And we must learn to seek his wisdom to help us curb the sins of speech. This area of our Christian life, more than any other, can keep us from the goal of Christian maturity.

I received a letter from a friend working for a missionary organization in Europe. He wrote, 'We are mainly well. The work at the conference centre is going very well *because I am dealing with things and not people*: mowing the lawn, fixing furniture, repairing electrical cords or machines.' Relationships to things are so much less susceptible to difficulties because they do not involve our tongues. The most powerful force hindering our quest for maturity is the misuse of words. What words are we using habitually, and what effect are they having on our actions and relationships? It is not just a matter of speaking positive words; it is dealing by repentance with the negative ones. Is there someone I need to apologize to? Is there a broken relationship I need to mend?

Given the unruly nature of the tongue, self-help techniques will surely fail. If we want control of what we say, then we must look elsewhere. It is a matter of looking to the Lord for help and praying, as the psalmist prays: 'Set a guard over my mouth, O LORD; keep watch over the door of my lips' (Ps. 141:3).

# 16.
# The two wisdoms

*Please read James 3:13-18*

On one holiday I visited the Royal Australian Air Force museum at Point Cook in my home state of Victoria. Two or three times a week the museum puts on a flying display of one of their vintage aircraft. An aircraft is brought out from the hangar and the pilot gives a talk and answers questions about the plane before taking off and demonstrating its capabilities in the air. On that day the aircraft was a Winjeel (an aboriginal word meaning 'young eagle'), a locally produced training machine built in the 1950s. The pilot was a senior officer with a lifetime of service and thousands of hours of flying experience. Before taking the plane up, he told us that this aircraft was very unstable when taxiing. In particular it had a tendency to do what was called a ground loop, in which the tail of the aircraft would spin around and the pilot would end up going in the opposite direction to the one he wanted. It didn't matter how experienced he was; he could still end up making a fool of himself. He added that there were only two kinds of pilots who flew this aircraft: those who had done a ground loop and those who were about to do one.

We could say something similar about the Christian life. We never become so expert or so accomplished in the

Christian life that we become free from making mistakes or acting foolishly. There are Christians who have committed acts of folly, and there are those who are about to. James has just shown us that our folly is nowhere better demonstrated than in the use of the tongue (3:2-12). This is all the more critical for those who become teachers in the church (3:1). An offhand remark, a careless comment, a thoughtless word, or an unwise application of Scripture can have such a disastrous affect that it can undo months, or even years, of an otherwise fruitful teaching ministry.

So it is in this context that James gives us much-needed advice on wisdom. We need wisdom in what we say, because our tongues so often get us into trouble. But we also need wisdom for every part of life. We desperately need God's help in order to conduct ourselves wisely in this world. The question in verse 13 introduces the main theme of this section, which is wisdom and understanding: **'Who is wise and understanding among you?'**

Then, in what follows, James gives a description of two kinds of wisdom. He does this by way of contrast. There is a wisdom that comes from heaven, which is spiritual and divine; there is also a wisdom that is earthly, unspiritual and devilish. We might have expected James to contrast wisdom with folly at this point, since this is the contrast that the Old Testament Wisdom books like Proverbs and later Jewish Wisdom writers normally make. But he does not use the word 'folly' (even though it is folly), instead choosing to describe an alternative kind of wisdom, a false one. I think this is deliberate. Life is rarely, if ever, black and white. The devil doesn't come along and say to us, 'Believe this lie and be damned.' What is folly is not always recognized as folly. It sometimes masquerades as wisdom, a counterfeit wisdom — one that is actually earthly, unspiritual and of the devil.

The wisdom from below is sometimes subtle and not always easy to discern. In fact, says James, it is easier to spot it by its fruit than by its form. In other words, if we are not sure whether something is wise or unwise we are to look at the results. If there is growing godliness, a harvest of righteous living and the formation of a loving and pastorally caring community, we are seeing **'the wisdom that comes from heaven'** at work (3:17); on the other hand, **'disorder and every evil practice'** (3:16) are sure signs of false wisdom.

## Who is wise and understanding? (3:13)

Wisdom is an indispensable element of the Christian life. We have already seen that wisdom is a gift that God promises to believers to help them face trials (1:5-8). But even a superficial glance at the disarray in many churches should be enough to convince us that when it comes to wisdom there is a distinct vacuum. However, when James asks the question, **'Who is wise and understanding among you?'** we would probably all put our names forward with all the humility we can muster. I doubt that any one of us would think of ourselves as foolish. We tend to think of ourselves as thoughtful and astute, though, if pressed, we might admit to having done some silly things. But the question put by James should at least force us to ponder more deeply what wisdom is and where it is to be found.

When James says, **'Let him show it by his good life ...'**, we are alerted to the fact that wisdom cannot be limited to knowing; it is manifest in *doing*. If there is a heresy of belief, so also there is a heresy of life. The former happens when we believe and teach wrong things about God; the latter when we fail to show what we know of God by our **'life'** (i.e. deeds).

Furthermore, the 'good life' must be accompanied by an attitude of **'humility'**. This quality is not innate to us. What is commanded here is not morality or a self-help religion, but rather a virtue that comes through faith in Christ. So we need to look to him for help.


**Wisdom from below** (3:14-16)

Firstly, James gives a horrible picture of how things can go wrong in the church where wisdom is lacking (3:16). Probably we have all known churches like this — where there is an absence of brotherly affection, or where Christians are treating one another badly. To the shame of the church there is a loss of trust; friends become alienated; a root of bitterness creeps in, and congregations are torn apart.

What does James say is the cause? It is not the structures of the church, nor the system, nor church politics. It doesn't happen without reason. James traces it back to a wisdom from below which he describes as **'earthly, unspiritual, of the devil'**. In particular he mentions the two telltale signs of this kind of wisdom.

The first is **'bitter envy'** (3:14). Envy (or jealousy) is a sin that quickly disrupts the harmony of the church. It can arise when others challenge our ideas or we lose influence (Acts 5:17; 13:45).

**'Selfish ambition'**, the second characteristic of earthly wisdom mentioned by James, is very much the evil twin of envy. It is self-seeking — the quest for personal gain or power. The promotion of self and the desire for recognition mean that a person thinks more highly of himself than he ought. Consequently he is easily offended by those who do not share his sense of importance. The result is rivalry, often leading to factionalism. The body of Christ prospers when its members work together in the 'unity of the Spirit', not when they view each other competitively. In Scripture we can read of a church leader called Diotrephes who loved to be first

(3 John 9). Do we genuinely find satisfaction in the successes and advancement of others?

The hidden qualities of bitter envy and selfish ambition find their outlet in unwise words such as boasting (3:14). But craving recognition from our peers, or constantly comparing ourselves with them, is a sure sign of wisdom from below. Paul wrote to the chaotic Corinthian church, 'We do not dare to classify or compare ourselves with some who commend themselves. When they measure themselves by themselves and compare themselves with themselves, they are not wise' (2 Cor. 10:12). If we are to boast then let it not be in ourselves, but in the Lord (1 Cor. 1:31).

A boastful kind of wisdom is earthly, being tied to the thinking and standards of this world, and it is unspiritual because it has never been touched and sanctified by the gracious operations of the Spirit of God. Finally, it is of the devil (3:15). As the tide of gospel influence in the West recedes, we increasingly fail to recognize and take account of the reality of the devil, but James had no such blind spot. He introduces us to a parallel but unseen spirit world whose influence impinges upon our own material one. There is a malevolent spirit which seeks to destroy the work of God by promoting false wisdom.

**Wisdom from heaven** (3:17-18)

What is true wisdom, and how do we obtain it? It is probably better to start by stating what it is not. It is not a natural endowment, nor is it linked to our IQ. It is not inherited from our parents or genetically transmitted through their genes. A clever person may or may not have it. James indicates that the source of this wisdom is **'from heaven'** (3:17), thereby excluding all earthly origins. It comes from God (1:5) and resides in God. It is one of his attributes. Job says, 'To God belong wisdom and power' (Job 12:13). God's wisdom is supremely displayed in Christ, who is 'the power of God and the wisdom of God' (1 Cor. 1:24).

But wisdom is not just a divine attribute; it is a communicable one. There is a gift of wisdom which we can receive and which God wants his people to demonstrate in their lives (3:13). We need it to help us control our speech, to face life's moral dilemmas and difficult choices, to face trials with joy, to cope with the increasing isolation of old age, to face unexpected poverty and to deal with lasting regrets, missed opportunities, past hurts, disappointments and disobedience. There is not a believer who is not in need of the wisdom from above for each day. We need it in the church, to minister without causing offence except that of the gospel, to avoid unnecessary conflict and to mutually submit to one another in the Lord. Every day brings its own particular challenges.

This wisdom resides in God and has been communicated to us propositionally in his Word. When the Holy Spirit takes that word and applies it to our hearts, then we have wisdom to live by and to die by. The question then arises: 'How do we know if we have received this wisdom?' James answers, not by giving us a definition of wisdom, but by describing the attitudes, qualities and works it produces. His description is remarkably similar to Paul's elaboration of the fruit of the Spirit (Gal. 5:22-23). Indeed, wisdom in the letter of James, though not identical with the Holy Spirit, acts as the functional equivalent of the role that the Holy Spirit plays in sanctification in Paul's writings. This should not be surprising in a letter which is given over for the most part to helping us become more Christlike in character in all that we do, think and desire.

Wisdom from heaven is **'first of all pure'** (3:17). This is not just first sequentially. By **'first'** James means that the overarching quality of the wisdom from above is purity.

These days many people are concerned about purity. We want an environment that is clean, air that is pure and free from smoke and radiation; we want foods that are free from harmful chemicals and manufacturing additives. 'Organically grown' is a common sales pitch to the health-minded. But are we as concerned about the purity of the things we think, say or do? God's desire is for a pure church, pure in its worship, its teaching, its fellowship and its service (Eph. 5:27). Though that purity is not something that will ever be perfectly achieved in this life, nevertheless it is his goal for us.

The following characteristics help us to recognize the wisdom from heaven.

### 1. 'Peace-loving'

Paul in Ephesians says we are to make every effort to keep the unity of the Spirit in the bond of peace (Eph. 4:3). This wisdom loves peace by overlooking minor offences, not dwelling on unhappy incidents, not allowing a root of bitterness to develop, listening patiently to others, quickly forgiving, not insisting on its own way, not being quickly angered — all of which are in fact the qualities of love outlined in 1 Corinthians 13:4-7.

### 2. 'Considerate'

Wisdom that loves peace is also **'considerate'**, knowing how to make allowances for people. Not everyone has had the advantage of a stable, loving home, together with exposure to the Scriptures from their youth. Perhaps they have not reached the level of Christian maturity that others have. The considerate person shows 'gentleness', as Jesus did (2 Cor. 10:1). He exemplified this trait when dealing with the lost and straying, showing kindness and compassion to those whose lives were in a muddle.

### 3. 'Submissive' ('open to reason', RSV)

The Greek word (*eupeithēs*) only occurs here in the New Testament (something technically known as a hapax legomenon) and does not derive from the family of words normally translated as **'submissive'** (as the NIV renders it). So the word may be better understood according to its literal meaning, 'open to reason', as in the RSV. The idea is that of someone who is willing to listen to another point of view. This doesn't mean we are to have no convictions or to hold no firm opinions. Clearly when core gospel issues are at stake we are to be unyielding. Paul was willing to be all things to all men (1 Cor. 9:22; 10:33) but his willingness to accommodate others was not boundless. When he came to Corinth he refused to preach the cross of Christ with eloquent wisdom lest the content of the gospel message should be compromised by the manner in which it was conveyed (1 Cor. 1:17). The opposite idea is that of someone who is obstinate, with a closed mind. 'Open to reason' suggests that we are open to a fresh view on issues and to change our opinion when wrong.

### 4. 'Full of mercy and good fruit'

**'Mercy'** is a word that has been used before (2:13). It is love for a neighbour demonstrated in practical ways (2:8). James also provides an example of what mercy looks like (albeit negatively), for if the man who claimed to have faith had been full of mercy then he would have met the need of the poorly clothed and ill-fed brother or sister (2:14-16). Mercy is deliberately linked with **'good fruit'** to emphasize the wholesome and productive nature of genuine wisdom.

## 5. *'Impartial'*

We have already met this quality in chapter 2:1-7. It is to treat people equally, without consideration of social status or personal benefit.

## 6. *'Sincere'*

In computing terms WYSIWYG is an acronym for 'What you see is what you get'. It refers to the expectation that the document you see on your computer monitor will be exactly the one your printer produces. In human terms the equivalent is being **'sincere'**. We are to be transparent in our intentions and without guile in our motives. When heavenly wisdom is absent there is a lack of integrity (WYSINWYG).

The application of all this is found in verse 18, where James uses an agricultural metaphor to teach that righteousness is a harvest reaped by those **'who sow in peace'**. In other words, if we want to see righteous living in the church, instead of seeing 'disorder and every evil practice', we need an environment of peace. Our calling, then, is to be peacemakers as well as peacekeepers (cf. Matt. 5:9).

# 17.
# The problem of worldliness



There is an Indian story about the great archer Arjuna and his skill with the bow and arrow. A guru had set up a target — a wooden bird — in a tree and asked his three pupils what they saw. One said, 'The forest'; the next said, 'Trees'; but Arjuna said, 'The bird's eye.' His prowess as an archer came from seeing the essentials. James fires his arrow at 'the bird's eye' of what was the core issue among the churches of the diaspora — worldliness. Worldliness is the elevation of someone or something above or alongside God in our lives. The primary symptom of worldliness is pride, which comes from a refusal to accept our status as creatures and consequently our dependence on God. We behave as though we were masters of our own lives and destinies (cf. 4:13-17).

James is picking up the thread of a theme that is familiar by now — his readers' immaturity. The cause of their lack of progress is that they want only enough of Christ to be saved, not disturbed; they affirm orthodoxy, but do not see it as life-changing; though they value the law's morality, they fail to wage war against the inner pollution of the heart; they delight in the teaching of God's Word, yet are not careful with their own words; they love to listen to sermons, but fail to practise what they hear; and, despite believing in the power of prayer, they find their own prayer life unrewarding and empty. These are the fruits of compromise with the world. It is perfectly possible to maintain an outward, formal relationship with God while inwardly cultivating idolatrous passions.

## Symptoms of worldliness (4:1-3)

Worldliness is commonly associated with an external set of standards of behaviour. For a past generation of Christians, being an evangelical was defined by a certain code of conduct. The avoidance of such things as smoking, alcohol, or wearing make-up, and 'no-go' areas, like the pub, dance-hall or cinema, provided a benchmark of separation from 'the world'. A new, postmodern generation of believers, however, does not know or care about the shibboleths of a past 'evangelical' lifestyle. So we must return to Scripture and examine afresh the root of worldliness. According to James, worldliness is an issue of the heart before it becomes a lifestyle. Other Scriptures take a similar view (1 John 2:16). It is the yielding to evil desires that war within our hearts (4:1). Worldliness is recognized less by what one does than by what one loves.

Chronic failure to get on with other Christians is the first symptom of worldliness (4:1). James exposes the problem of disunity by asking a rhetorical question which is couched in the language of strife: **'What causes fights and quarrels among you?'** The answer to it is provided by a question in the second part of the verse, **'Don't they come from your desires that battle within you?'**, which is phrased in such a way as to expect the answer, 'Yes.' James' explanation refers to the inner life, to the unseen and conflicting **'desires'** within the human heart. When a newsreader announces an 'outbreak of war' in some part of the world, what he is really talking about is an 'inbreak of war'. The point that James makes is that there is an inner war before there is an outward war. War has its origins in the human heart; hence he makes a connection between the inner self and its competing sinful desires and the many outward projections of those inner sinful desires.

In other words, the basic motivation in war is not politics, though politics contribute. Expanding populations and a consequent scarcity of food as a source of violent conflict are not the cause, as some might think. No, the unpalatable truth is much nearer to home. It is because of the activity of the sinful desires of the human heart, more narrowly described here in terms of passion, pride and worldliness. This is where the gospel offers a remedy. If the problem starts within, we must deal with it at that point. It is no good treating the symptom; we must treat the cause. If the problem is the heart, we must change the heart, which is what the gospel of our Lord Jesus Christ comes to do. The remedy for war is ultimately a gospel remedy.

Of course James is not primarily speaking of wars between nations or peoples. He is addressing disunity **'among you'** — that is, within the church and between Christians. None the less, the root causes are the same, though in a different setting and on a smaller scale. James is describing believers engaged in strife with each other, a scenario for which he offers us both an analysis and a solution. Our sinful desires campaign within our hearts to gain mastery (4:1). They also clash with other people's desires (4:2). This causes ugly behaviour ranging from friction to feuding.

These verses place the onus for disunity squarely on our own doorstep. Responsibility for discord is personal. An inclination to fight is not generated by an unhappy home, a violent neighbourhood or bad companions. These things might aggravate the problem, but they do not cause it. Our desires are our own. We need to acknowledge them and repent of them where appropriate.

Verses 2 and 3 expand on the effect of letting our passions dominate us. Frustrated desire can lead to destructive behaviour, including murder (**'you kill and covet'**). Wanting something badly enough can lead to the actual taking of a life, as we see with King Ahab, who coveted Naboth's vineyard in 1 Kings 21. But is James suggesting that the Christians in view here were actually killing each other? After all, King Ahab was not noted for his trust in the Lord and this is a New Testament letter to Christians. Some commentators believe that the verb **'kill'** here should be taken literally, because this is its normal meaning, and suggest that some of the first readers might have been zealots who used violence in the name of religion. This conclusion is unnecessary. For one thing, zealots didn't usually kill each other. In any case, the word can have a spiritual sense, as it does in the teaching of Jesus, from whom James draws so much of his material (Matt. 5:21-26). Besides, these were brothers in Christ (**'among you'**), among whom no record of violent behaviour is found elsewhere in the New Testament. At the very most the language is hyperbole, pointing to murder as an end point — a result which in reality would never be observed. Far more often frustrated desires lead us to murder someone in our hearts (Matt. 5:21-22). These passions fuel a desire to destroy a person's reputation with angry words; thus church disunity often starts with criticism, backbiting, accusation, or slander.

The other symptom of worldliness is a neglected or unfulfilling prayer life (4:2-3). The purpose of prayer is that we might receive good things from God. He attaches promises to his encouragements to pray (Matt. 6:5-6; Luke 11:9-13; John 16:24; 1 John 5:14-15). Yet blessings may be withheld when prayer is neglected: **'You do not have, because you do not ask God'** (4:2). We do not go to God and do not talk to him about what we need. James puts it in the plainest possible language.

> Oh what peace we often forfeit,
> Oh what needless pain we bear,
> All because we do not carry,
> Everything to God in prayer!
>
> (Joseph Scriven, 1819–1886).

Where covetousness is the motivation, prayer is frustrated: **'When you ask, you do not receive, because you ask with wrong motives...'** (4:3). The disunity that troubles the church is furthered by a kind of prayer which is no prayer at all. It has the form of prayer, yet denies its power. It sounds like prayer, but the Lord who sees the heart sees that it is offered simply to satisfy selfish desires. It is not at all interested in submitting to him or his Word. We talk about a glass ceiling, which refers to situations where promotion in an organization is limited by some form of discrimination, which may be to do with race, gender, religion, or nepotism. There is also a stained-glass ceiling found in the church, where a person's prayer does not rise to the throne of grace because of wrong motives. All the indicators show that worldly people may also be prayerful people; nevertheless their prayers remain unanswered.

## God's opposition to worldliness (4:4)

Of all the many ways in which James addresses his readers, the one he uses here, **'you adulterous people'**, is the most forceful. It is the clue to understanding what he finds most lacking in his readers. The major cause of spiritual immaturity and the withholding of God's blessing is **'friendship with the world'** (4:4).

Few actions endanger the marriage bond more than adultery, which has a spiritual equivalent in the church. The expression **'adulterous people'** conveys a picture of marital breakdown. It is a term that goes back to the Old Testament, where the relationship between God and his people is compared to the marriage bond (e.g. Isa. 54:5; Jer. 3:20). This background lies behind the Lord's command to the prophet Hosea to marry a prostitute (Hosea 1:2). What a scandalous sign to the people of Israel of their unfaithfulness! The same concept is used by Jesus of those who rejected him, when he calls them 'a wicked and adulterous generation' (Matt. 12:39). One of the New Testament metaphors for the church is the bride of Christ (Eph. 5:32). The marriage relationship is completed when the New Jerusalem (the people of God) comes down out of heaven as a bride adorned for her husband (Rev. 21:2).

If we are members of the church we are the bride of Christ. We belong to him absolutely, exclusively and sacrificially. And we are to be wholly faithful to him in our love and service. It would be unthinkable to cultivate other lovers. How well do our lives, our values, our thinking, our speaking reflect this exclusive marriage bond? We may never have been guilty of sexual unfaithfulness, but has there been spiritual adultery? Are there other lovers in our lives?

The main burden James has for his readers, and the most pressing concern in his writing, is to warn them of divided loyalties. A love triangle had developed, and James addresses it very directly. He says that we cannot be friends with the world. If we do, we make an enemy of God.

**Encouragements to avoid worldliness** (4:5-6)

Christians use different translations of the Bible. Occasionally this can lead to some interesting discussions when translators disagree on how a particular verse is to be rendered. Verse 5 is a prime example, the issue being whether the words 'envy' and 'spirit' refer to man or God.

    1. Human envy, and the spirit as the human spirit (see Gen. 2:7):**'Or do you think Scripture says without reason that the spirit he caused to live in us envies intensely?'** (4:5, NIV — cf. GNT, NAB).

    2. Divine envy and the spirit as the Holy Spirit: 'Or do you think that the Scripture speaks to no purpose: "He jealously desires the Spirit which he has made to dwell in us"?' (4:5, NASB — cf. NKJV, LB)

If it is human envy, then the sentence refers to our tendency to covet and be jealous of other people. That is the normal way of understanding the word 'envy'. However, if it is divine envy, then it refers to the Lord's desire for the best love and principal loyalty of our hearts. It is difficult to decide on linguistic grounds, but the context is determinative, pointing towards the idea of divine jealousy, and the spirit therefore as being the Holy Spirit. Jealousy is an appropriate response should a husband find his wife flirting with another man (or vice versa). Worldliness is regarded by the Lord as spiritual adultery (4:4) and he is rightly outraged by it.

The other difficulty with this same verse is identifying which Old Testament text James is drawing from when he asks, **'Or do you think Scripture says ...?'** Although the Old Testament speaks of the Lord's jealousy for his people in many places (e.g. Exod. 20:5; 34:14, Deut. 4:24; 5:9; 6:15), no one text matches exactly the one we have here. Hence it is more likely that **'Scripture'** here refers to the general theme of the Lord's jealousy in the Old Testament rather than to a particular verse.

There is a wonderful encouragement in this verse regarding the depth of God's love for us. He who planned our redemption and who, in the fulness of time, sent his Son to accomplish it also sent his Spirit to dwell in our hearts. And he who dwells in us is at work within us with unwearied patience to present us before God without spot or blemish. He yearns jealously over every part of our lives, and so if we court the friendship of the world we cause his jealousy. Paul writes in a similar way about the activity of the Spirit opposing the sinful nature (Gal. 5:17). We are to remember, when the world beckons and we find ourselves attracted, that there is another opposing 'passion' aroused. We must not fool ourselves into thinking that God does not mind when other interests and affections diminish our love for him. His jealousy is aroused.

In verse 6 we have another great 'but' of Scripture: **'But he gives us more grace.'** As the attractions and distractions of the world threaten to overwhelm us and sweep us away, grace is given so that we may withstand their influence. As the strength of temptation increases, more grace is given to meet it.

The grace spoken of here is not the irresistible grace of salvation, but the grace to overcome worldliness and to grow to maturity. It is grace given to the humble in heart. James reminds us of this by another Scripture reference — this time to a specific passage: **'God opposes the proud, but gives grace to the humble'** (Prov. 3:34, also quoted in 1 Peter 5:5). The text confronts us with our natural tendency to be proud.

Pride is a characteristic of worldliness, arising from our rebellion against the creator God and our refusal to acknowledge our utter dependence on him. It is an illogical condition since all that we have and are has been given to us by God (1 Cor. 4:7). Pride causes God's wrath, and he opposes it (Ps. 18:27; Prov. 6:17; 16:5). Humility is both the opposite of pride and the condition for receiving grace. Humility is not a work of merit; it is seen in the empty hand stretching out to God in recognition of our creaturely status and reliance on him for all our needs. To those who are humble God gives grace. This grace is the pathway to usefulness for Christ and blessing for his church. Our failures cannot be excused by special pleading, by our lack of natural talent, or by unfavourable circumstances. The cause is rather our stubbornness and pride. Of humility much more needs to be said, but James reserves that for the next section (4:7-10).

In this life sin is never fully eradicated from the heart even though it may no longer have dominion. This makes us vulnerable to worldliness at any time. Even when we truly love Christ and long to serve him we may find our affections wandering. Other 'lovers' beckon, and we are flattered by their attentions. In the light of James' warnings against worldliness, are there any loves in our lives that are in danger of becoming idols? Do we love Jesus today more than we did a year ago? Is there someone in the church whom we are 'battling' against, or 'avoiding'? (Some 'battles' are necessary because they involve core gospel issues; if so, are we conducting them with genuine Christian grace and charity?) Is our prayer life empty and frustrating? Are we still as enthusiastic about our fellowship with other Christians, or have we withdrawn somewhat?

# 18.
# The remedy for worldliness

*Please read James 4:7-10*

There is a story about a church member who was recognized for his humble service. As an acknowledgement he was given a pin badge to wear. The next Sunday he wore it to church, whereupon it was immediately taken away from him because he was proud! William Law wrote, 'You can have no greater sign of a confirmed pride than when you think you are humble enough.' If we consider ourselves to be humble, then we are not. It is an unselfconscious virtue. The irony of humility is that those who really possess it do not have the slightest idea that they do so. Even to draw attention to this quality seems inappropriate, since it is such a delicate flower. Yet the Bible speaks a lot about the need for humility and the possibility of attaining it (e.g. 2 Chr. 7:14; Ps. 25:9; Prov. 15:33; Eph. 4:2; Phil. 2:3).

But humility is not the most sought-after virtue in society, even though it might be a quality we admire in others. It is a trait that will not get us noticed, is often confused with weakness, goes against us in job interviews, and will not procure us service in a crowded shop. Uriah Heep was a character invented by Charles Dickens in the novel *David Copperfield* who ingratiated himself with people, wringing his hands and coming alongside them, saying with false modesty, 'I am well aware that I am the 'umblest person going.'[1] Clearly he was not humble at all!

The word **'then'** ('therefore', RSV) in verse 7 connects worldliness (4:1-6) with humility (4:7-10). The answer to worldliness is therefore humility. Though not so obvious in our English translations, the striking feature of verses 7-10 is the number of commands given. There are ten of them (**'submit'**, **'resist'**, **'come near'**, **'wash'**, **'purify'**, **'grieve'**, **'mourn'**, **'wail'**, **'change'**, **'humble ...'**). Despite the variety of commands, the overarching theme is humility. The section begins and ends with this idea: **'Submit yourselves, then, to God... Humble yourselves before the Lord...'**

The beginning of humility is submission to God, which is not a popular concept in an egalitarian society (i.e. 'We are all equal'), because it implies inferiority. Instead we are told to assert ourselves, blow our own trumpet, stand up for our rights, and more. But submission is related to *role*, not necessarily to *nature*. We are told that Jesus '... being in very nature God ... humbled himself' and took on the role of a servant' (Phil. 2:6-8). Submission to God was supremely exemplified by our Lord, whose incarnation involved emptying himself and submitting to his Father's will. His earthly life involved submission. From childhood (Luke 2:51) to the cross (Luke 22:42), he complied with those who had authority over him. He summarized his earthly ministry by saying that he had come not to be served but to serve and to give his life as a ransom for many (Mark 10:45). If submission lies at the heart of Christ, should we not follow his pattern of service? Can it be such a surprise if otherwise our service is feeble and fruitless? Those who really submit to God have no personal agenda. Like Jesus, their will is to do the Father's will.

The Christian recognizes that there are additional dimensions to submission. True submission lies outside our natural abilities, requiring the grace of God. Besides the acknowledgement that God is God and that we are creatures, there is the wonder of God's continuing mercy in Christ towards us as sinners. James Hamilton comments: 'Humility is the grace that lies prostrate at God's footstool, self-abasing and self-disparaging, amazed at God's mercy and abhorring its own vileness.' As we progress towards maturity, there is an increasing consciousness of the depth of our sinfulness, the lack of a Christlike character and a mounting debt to the mercy of God. We live, but only because Christ lives in us; we serve, but only because of the grace of God; as we submit to God, the more we become aware of our poverty of spirit (Matt. 5:3); and we are never more truly 'in character' as Christians than when, like Paul, we confess ourselves to be 'the worst of sinners' (1 Tim. 1:16).

## Three commands with a promise (4:7-10)

Three of the commands in verses 7 to 10 are directly joined to promises and can be set out as follows:

| *Command* | *Promise* | |
|---|---|---|
| Resist the devil | and he will flee from you | (4:7) |
| Come near to God | and he will come near to you | (4:8) |
| Humble yourselves before the Lord | and he will lift you up | (4:10) |

We shall consider each of these in turn.

*1. 'Resist the devil, and he will flee ...' (4:7)*

The command to **'resist'** introduces a new element — the devil. Worldly Christians are of little interest to the devil, unlike humble and repentant ones.

The devil is referred to in nineteen of the twenty-seven books of the New Testament, and nearly always in relation to his hostility towards the church or individual believers. Any consideration of evil which does not take account of his activity is lacking. Of course some take an unhealthy interest in his activities and ascribe to him powers that are not his to wield, while others are fascinated by the extraordinary phenomena associated with demon possession. Most in the West, influenced by a materialistic world view, under-estimate or ignore him.

The Bible presents us with a view of the physical world as constantly interacting with, and influenced by, spiritual powers — some good and some evil. We cannot see these powers, but they exist and have an effect on our lives. In the previous section we were reminded of the good influence of the Holy Spirit, who indwells the believer (4:5). He reveals the truth of God, unites believers to Christ, assures us of our adoption, intercedes for us, prompts the churches' mission and, as 'the Spirit of wisdom' (Isa.11:2), progressively transforms us into the likeness of Christ through trials. But there are also evil powers subject to one who is called the devil.

The command is to **'resist the devil'** (4:7). Resistance implies defence. In other words, we don't go out and pick a fight with him, but rather we are to recognize his work and take a stand against him. His activity can be identified from the various names he is given in Scripture. He is called the 'accuser' of the brethren (Rev. 12:10), the 'father of lies' (John 8:44) and, here, **'the devil'**, which means 'slanderer'. A slanderer is someone who uses words to discredit and destroy the reputation and integrity of another. The devil will seek to exploit the evil desires within us to stir up fights and quarrels (4:1). He softly whispers of the unfairness of others towards us and panders to our wounded pride. We respond with a fiery tongue, and are quick to demolish the character of people made in the image of God (3:9). James deals more thoroughly with the topic of slander in the next section (4:11-12).

If we resist the devil, we shall find the promise true that **'he will flee from you'**. Resistance is possible because the devil is a defeated foe. The battle between God and the devil is not a cosmic struggle the outcome of which lies in the balance and is uncertain. We resist one who has been mortally wounded by Christ's work on the cross (John 12:31).

## 2. *'Come near to God and he will come near to you'* (4:8-9)

The promise, **'He will come near to you'**, offers intimate fellowship with our Creator and Redeemer. Although this promise has been used in evangelism, that is not its intent. It is a text for believers who want to deepen their communion with the Lord. Relationships such as marriage have their ups and downs, and so too does the Christian life. The believer sometimes feels that God is far away. He is always near, but our experience of that is not always constant. William Cowper expresses the sense of loss the believer sometimes feels:

> Oh, for a closer walk with God,
> A calm and heav'nly frame;
> A light to shine upon the road
> That leads me to the Lamb!
>
> Where is the blessedness I knew
> When first I saw the Lord?

Where is the soul-refreshing view
Of Jesus and his word?
                              (William Cowper, 1731–1800).

We draw near to God by repentance from sin (generally) and double-mindedness (specifically), as the ensuing commands suggest (4:8). Both commands recall Old Testament instructions for drawing near to God in worship. The first is, **'Wash your hands, you sinners'** (cf. Exod. 30:20-21), and the second, **'Purify your hearts, you double-minded'** (cf. Ps. 24:3-4).

After targeting the purely intellectual faith of some of his readers, James next issues a set of commands referring to the physical and emotional responses that accompany repentance, which are grief, mourning and weeping (4:9). In the pattern of the prophets, he calls his readers to a godly sorrow 'that leads to salvation and leaves no regret' (2 Cor. 7:10).

Notice that all of these commands are plural, suggesting that the repentance in view is that of the whole church (though the individual is not excluded). By comparison, contemporary gatherings for worship are usually thought to be lacking if they are not lively and 'fun'. Of course, it is a delight to worship God because of his surpassing excellence, and at the heart of worship lies the redemptive provision that God has graciously afforded us in Christ. But if deeply felt repentance is absent from our worship, are we not failing to draw near to God? Worship incorporates both rejoicing and repentance.

*3. 'Humble yourselves ... and he will lift you up' (4:10)*

The puzzle of verse 10 is not the command to **'humble yourselves'**, which has been stated before. It lies in the promise that follows: **'... and he will lift you up.'** Normally the verb 'to lift up' is associated with Christ's exaltation, not ours. In Christ we have the perfect example of the one who received this promise. His obedience unto death was a humiliation. In resurrection and ascension he was raised to the highest position of all (Phil. 2:9). But how does this promise apply to us? What does it mean for *us* to be lifted up?

The idea of God lifting up the humble (as well as bringing down the proud) is an Old Testament theme repeated more than once in the New Testament. Peter repeats the promise here, as well as quoting from the same Old Testament passage (1 Peter 5:5-6). When Mary rejoiced in God as Saviour she picked up this reversal theme (Luke 1:46-55). To be 'lifted up' in the latter passage means to receive the grace of God in Christ and his blessing of salvation. God raises up the sinner who repents (the context suggests repentance from worldliness) and gives him the status of being right with God, making him part of his glorious kingdom and giving him a hope and a future.

> When God intends to fill a soul, he first makes it empty.
>
> When he intends to enrich a soul, he first makes it poor.
>
> When he intends to exalt a soul, he first makes it sensible to its own miseries, wants and nothingness
>
> (John Flavel, 1627–1691).

# 19.
# Speak no evil



Previously we saw that the signs of a worldly church are disunity (4:1), covetousness (4:2) and outward piety that conceals selfish motives (4:3). These things hinder growth, compromise our witness, grieve the Spirit and give the devil a foothold. But none of them is as symptomatic of worldliness as misuse of the tongue. James returns to the topic of self-control with respect to our speech (cf. 1:26; 3:1-12). A fluorescent highlighter would be less effective in drawing our attention to this topic than the manner and frequency of references to it in this letter. Where do we more need to know the help of God, submission to his Word and the restraint of the Spirit of Christ than in our speech? We may be able to mask many of the faults that mar our lives, but that feral member of our bodies — the tongue — is not so easily hidden (3:1-12). The words we speak offer a transparent window into the invisible room of the heart, exposing the life of the inner self.

The prohibition, **'Do not slander one another'**, is translated in various ways:

'Do not speak evil' (NKJV).
'Never pull each other to pieces' (J. B. Philips).

'Do not backbite one another' (Wycliffe).

The differences in translation help us to grasp the purpose of the command. We must not indulge in malicious gossip about others, or speak harshly so as to put them down, or take pleasure in exposing their faults. We are not to deliberately create a false impression about them by withholding some of the facts. An intentional half-truth is as much an untruth as a falsehood. Those we injure in this way are **'brothers'** (4:11), yet the hallmark of genuine fraternal relations is love (John 13:34).

The continuous tense of the verb can be rendered: 'Do not keep on slandering one another.' The effect of translating it in this way is clumsy, but the intent is clear. This is not a one-off injunction. Constant vigilance is necessary. The command is always contemporary, always relevant. Some are addicted to drink, some to gambling and others to pornography. While we deplore the harmful anti-social behaviour these generate, or pity those so obsessed, hardly a murmur is raised when we use our tongues to speak evil. This misuse of speech is just as addictive and the results equally devastating. Helplines and counsellors exist to help those caught up in a wide variety of addictive kinds of behaviour, but no such service exists for the gossiper. Besides, how many would attend a 'Gossips Anonymous' group?

Hearing juicy titbits about others is a continual source of delight for many. The book of Proverbs compares gossip to tasty food: 'The words of the gossip are like choice morsels; they go down to a man's inmost parts' (Prov. 18:8). This human weakness is fed by sections of the media that exist simply to obtain another morsel of sleaze to satisfy the insatiable appetites of those so addicted. Gossip can come with a spiritual overlay. How often does prayer become nothing more than a source of tittle-tattle? 'We need to pray for brother X; his marriage is going through a bad patch.' Do we really want to pray for the couple, or is there a perverse pleasure in discussing the personal problems of others? The exposure of their follies can promote self-righteousness and lessen the pain of our own failures. This is a crying evil all too common in the church, destroying fellowship, alienating friends, creating divisions and breeding hypocrisy.

In these verses James gives three reasons for not speaking evil.

## 1. We judge the law (4:11)

Note the unusual way in which this sin is described. We might think slander is an offence against the person, and indeed it is. But in Scripture it is regarded as an offence against **'the law'**. James may be picking up parts of the Old Testament law (Lev. 19:16), or the law of Christ 'not to judge' others (Matt. 7:1), but more likely he has in mind 'the royal law' — to love one's neighbour as oneself (2:8).

The description of God as Lawgiver (4:12) is a reminder that we are called to live by his law. There is sometimes confusion about the place of the law in the Christian life. Some contend that we are no longer under law but under grace; therefore the Old Testament moral law enshrined in the Ten Commandments is no longer valid. Instead, they say, we are to live by the new commandment of love given by Jesus (John 13:34). Yet this is a misunderstanding of what Jesus taught about the law (Matt. 5:17-19). The Christian is not under law to be justified (i.e. for salvation), but to be guided by it for sanctification (i.e. for maturity). The moral law exposes our sin and reveals what God wants of us in order that, animated by the Spirit of Christ, we may learn to delight in what he delights in. None of this is contrary to the gospel, which frees us from the condemnation of the law.

Slander is an offence against the law. When we speak evil of one another we are taking a certain position with respect to the law. Instead of respecting it, sitting under it and seeking to obey it, we are in fact placing ourselves above it. We may never have thought of speaking evil in that way, but we need to view these matters as God views them. Every time we adopt a disparaging way of speaking about others, we reveal a superior attitude that suggests we know better than God's Word. Though we may say we hold a high doctrine of Scripture and profess to uphold its truth, speaking evil reveals a failure of practice. Doing what God's Word says shows we sit under the law as brothers and sisters in Christ.

## 2. We forget who God is (4:12)

The way we think about God matters. The Christian life is shaped by our conception of God's character. When James describes God as the **'one Lawgiver'**, the corresponding picture is of God's unique ('one') and supreme authority ('Lawgiver'). An integral part of this picture is the Judge, since in the legal system he is the one appointed to decide on matters of law, so we see that God is both the Lawgiver and the Judge, and this understanding of God provides a framework for understanding why slander is an offence.

God has given the law primarily to show us our sin and to point us to the gospel remedy in Christ: 'Through the law we become conscious of sin' (Rom. 3:20). The Spirit uses the law to convince us of sin, righteousness and judgement. We need to know against whom we have sinned and what sin justly deserves. Through the law we understand our sin and guilt before him who has the power both **'to save and destroy'** (4:12). The gospel must be framed within this context because the wonder of the gospel is that Christ has paid the penalty for our sins on the cross in order that by a penitent faith we might draw near to God. We must not shy away from this. We need to keep on coming back to the Lord, no matter how wretched we may feel over our sin and failure.

I am reminded of the poem by George Herbert (1593–1633):

> Love bade me welcome, yet my soul drew back,
> Guilty of dust and sin.
> But quick-ey'd Love, observing me grow slack
> From my first entrance in,
> Drew nearer to me, sweetly questioning
> If I lack'd anything.
>
> 'A guest,' I answer'd, 'worthy to be here';
> Love said, 'You shall be he.'
> 'I, the unkind, the ungrateful? Ah, my dear,
> I cannot look on thee.'
> Love took my hand, and smiling did reply,
> 'Who made the eyes but I?'
>
> 'Truth, Lord, but I have marr'd them; let my shame
> Go where it doth deserve.'
> 'And know you not,' says Love, 'who bore the blame?'
> 'My dear, then I will serve.'
> 'You must sit down,' says Love, 'and taste my meat.'
> So I did sit and eat.

## 3. We forget who we are (4:12)

The section concludes with a question expressing surprise and, indeed, outrage. The slander that makes us judges usurps the prerogative of the **'one Lawgiver'**. We violate his unique right as the Judge. He alone, and no other, has the right to determine the final spiritual destiny of every living person.

Making sweeping statements about others assumes a right and a knowledge which no one but God has. Who can know the heart like God does? To make a condemning statement about another is to take on a role for which we are eminently unqualified. A wife might leave her husband of many years. We may decry the act and speak of the sanctity of marriage and of the sacred promises she made 'for better or for worse', making the woman an object of scorn and criticism. Yet it may have been a difficult relationship. There may have been verbal, or even physical, abuse endured for many years. Family and friends 'in the know' would probably speak with far more restraint and love, but for the scandalmonger she is easy prey, an object of gossip. The simple truth is that we are not privy to all the facts. Even an earthly judge listens carefully and sifts the evidence before making a verdict, yet we can be quick to condemn, and unconcerned to know the other side of the story.

That is not to say that we must suspend our critical faculties. We are not required to be undiscerning and never hold an opinion. Nor does it mean that we are never to rebuke evil. James calls his readers 'adulterous' (4:4) and 'foolish' (2:20). John the Baptist referred to some would-be followers as a 'brood of vipers' (Matt. 3:7). Paul labels others who were perverting the gospel as 'dogs' and as doing 'evil' (Phil. 3:2). We are to recognize wrongdoing, but we are not to slander. We affirm that the person is God's image-bearer still and, as such, deserving of our respect.

## Conclusion

A speech therapist spends each day diagnosing and correcting speech problems people may have acquired through physical or cognitive disorders. James is a speech therapist of a different kind, seeking to correct a certain kind of speaking that has its origin in a spiritual malady. Typically, he traces the disorder to a defective view of God. While James restricts himself to analysing and correcting a speech problem, the rest of Scripture provides a rich source of help on how we should speak positively of and to each other.

If we are not to slander one another, what kind of speaking is encouraged? The following questions and Scripture references provide a brief reference framework:

*Is it true? Have I checked the facts?* 'These are the things you are to do: speak the truth to each other' (Zech. 8:16).

*Is it loving? Would I want the same said of me?* 'Instead, speaking the truth in love...' (Eph. 4:15); 'Love your neighbour as yourself' (James 2:8).

*Is it edifying? Does it build up?* 'Do not let any unwholesome talk come out of your mouths, but only what is helpful for building others up ... that it may benefit those who listen' (Eph. 4:29).

*Is it needful? Is it the right time and place?* 'Do not let any unwholesome talk come out of your mouths, but only what is helpful for building others up according to their needs (Eph. 4:29).

# 20.
# How to plan for the future



*Please read James 4:13-17*

We all have to face, and plan for, the future. People who don't make plans drift through life without direction or purpose. So we think ahead in order to achieve desirable and, it is to be hoped, God-honouring goals for ourselves. Failure to plan is often the reason for failure. Rebuking those who were planning a business venture might seem an unusual way of introducing a Bible passage. However, what James condemns is not so much the act of planning as the manner in which it is conducted. He is concerned not with planning for the future as such, but with *how* we make those plans.

The topic might have changed from slander to planning for the future, yet the underlying theme of worldliness is the same (4:1-10). Worldliness is the attempt by the creature to play god by throwing off dependence on the Creator. In the previous section (4:11-12) he played god by assuming the exclusive rights of the 'one Lawgiver' and becoming a judge. Here he plays god by imagining he can control his destiny. The same arrogance that judged others now presumes to have full control of life.

James is writing to churches that have a small number of wealthy businessmen, though most members of the congregation were probably struggling financially. Not many of us are wealthy entrepreneurs, so, even though the passage is addressing such people, we need to think about it in more general terms and apply it along the lines of 'How do we plan for our future?' Is there a way of looking ahead and of making preparation that avoids arrogance? How do we chart the future while at the same time acknowledging the Lord's sovereignty?

## How not to make a business plan (4:13)

A former missionary in Korea once told me that when the pastor of his church came to an important part of the sermon he would reach under his pulpit and ring a bell. This was a signal for the congregation to wake up and pay attention. The phrase **'now listen'** (4:13), unique to James (cf. 5:1), functions in like manner. James goes on to describe the typical business entrepreneur of his day.

Translated into modern terms, we have a description of the inner workings of a present-day boardroom. The directors are seated in leather chairs around a plush table while the CEO, with the aid of a mandatory power-point presentation, outlines the company's plan to open new markets. Slides are shown of the demographics; architectural drawings display new plant; spreadsheets indicate projected profit margins. It is a scene repeated daily throughout the corporate world. And for many business executives life consists of this. It is the heady world of numbers, profit, acquisitions, stock options, salary increments and keeping shareholders happy. Some are enslaved by such a lifestyle, which seems so necessary and so right, but Scripture has a different view.

Built into this corporate world view are four questionable presumptions:

1. The presumption of independent choice: **'Today or tomorrow we will go to…'**
2. The presumption of future prospects: **'spend a year there…'**
3. The presumption of performance ability: **'carry on business…'**
4. The presumption of material success: **'and make money…'**

It is a defective world view because it finds no place for God. When God is left out worldliness creeps in, and with it arrogant boasting. Clearly some of the businessmen in the early Christian church had imbibed this worldly culture and had made themselves a formidable enemy (4:4). But all of the above is equally applicable to any of us going about our work, however humble it may be. We are not to think of James' warning only in terms of the high-flying businessman.

**What planners forget** (4:14)

The tragedy of modern secular education is a curriculum that has become so crowded with courses of limited or novelty value that there is little place to consider the deeper issues of human existence. **'What is your life?'** is a question hardly ever considered. Indeed, there is a fear of asking it in case we disturb the equilibrium of plurality. The art of philosophizing about life has been moved off the curriculum and out of the classroom. But there has been a cost. Young people who need to understand about the world have not been helped, nor prepared for the trials and disappointments, or even the successes, of life. Australia, where I live, has one of the highest youth suicide rates in the world — the sad tip of an iceberg of unhappiness. An increasingly efficient life journey through a meaningless landscape (or, with the advent of the

Internet, a virtual one) produces frustration and dissatisfaction. No coherent framework is taught, and where there is lack of meaning, and the ability to control one's life turns out to be an illusion, it is no surprise that destructive behaviour occurs.

As an experiment I subscribed to a group offering advice on self-improvement. Among other things, I received the following pieces of advice:

- The dreams you hold in your heart but push to the back of your mind are within your reach. Accept the fact that you can create a better life.
- People are more than capable of creating compelling dreams, but the fear of failure often clouds the path. To avoid this pitfall, imagine that it is impossible to fail.
- As you begin taking steps towards the things you desire, you will meet with many obstacles along the way that have the potential to knock you off course for ever. To ensure this doesn't happen to you, answer the question: 'What's in it for me?'
- You are in control of your future and are the only one who can guarantee a better life.

Needless to say, there was no mention of God among any of these suggestions. The illusory power of positive thinking which undergirds the above advice cannot cope with human limitation and sinfulness. In a word, the advice is sheer arrogance.

James, by contrast, maintains that **'You do not even know what will happen tomorrow'** (4:14). We might reverently say that this is a generous time frame, since we do not even know what might happen today. The only time we can guarantee is the present. My life is my own only in the sense that I make choices for which I am responsible and accountable. Even then it is circumscribed by events over which I have no control. The future I must commit to the Lord. The psalmist expresses it beautifully when he says, 'My times are in your hands' (Ps. 31:15). In a sermon C. H. Spurgeon once said, 'There are two great certainties about things that shall come to pass — one is that God knows and the other is that we do not know.'

It is not just that my times are in his hand, but that they are brief times: **'a mist that appears for a little while and then vanishes'**. James draws on a common biblical theme of the uncertainty and frailty of human life (cf. Job 8:9; Ps. 103:15; Prov. 27:1; Isa. 40:6-8). As a student of the natural world, he has observed in the early morning the mist that lies low on the ground and fills the valley floor, giving the landscape a surreal appearance. Then the sun rises and it quickly **'vanishes'**. James is not even thinking of a life suddenly and tragically cut off in youth. Here is life lived out to the fullest extent. The tragedy of life, however, is not that it ends so soon, but that it ends without Christ.

> Life is short;
> death is sure.
> Sin is the curse;
> Christ is the cure
>
> (Mark Gedicks).

## An acknowledgement to make (4:15-16)

Verse 15 is the proof that James is not against planning for the future. The difference in this verse is that God is brought into the equation. In our planning there is to be a different attitude: **'Instead, you ought to say...'** The difference comes from the recognition that God is sovereign over the whole of life. He is not limited, as we are; nor is he ever overtaken by events. So we pray and plan. We humbly submit those plans to the greater wisdom of the Lord. We exercise reverent caution and develop a submissive attitude if our plans do not eventuate. Do we have that view? We need it for our evangelism, building projects, church growth, vocational decisions and all our relationships.

Although the formula, **'if it is the Lord's will'**, has come to be known as the 'Jacobean condition', it is misleading to think of it as exclusive to James. Christ taught his disciples to pray, 'Your will be done' (Matt. 6:10), and made this petition an essential element of all of our praying. In Gethsemane Jesus prayed, 'Yet not what I will, but what you will' (Mark 14:36). While Jesus was aware of his Father's will and did positively pray that it would be done, his trial of faith provides us with an example of submissive humility. It also reminds us of the struggle that it can be to do God's will, especially where suffering is involved and when self-will leads us in a contrary direction.

Should we say, 'if it is the Lord's will', every time we speak of the future? A formula often repeated loses its impact and significance. It can become a meaningless mantra rather than a sincere acknowledgment of God's sovereignty. Certainly we are not to say it in a fatalistic way, as some do, since that is a denial of personal responsibility and accountability. Rather, in saying it we consciously bring into our plans the acknowledgement that Jesus is Lord, that the future is his, that he is both good and wise and that, whatever happens, he can be trusted. The apostle Paul is a good example of a balanced approach regarding how to plan for the future, sometimes choosing to use James' formula or variations of it (e.g., Acts 18:21; Rom. 1:10; 1 Cor. 4:19), and at other times not (e.g., 2 Cor. 13:1; 2 Tim. 4:9; Titus 3:12).

## A proverb to remember (4:17)

Although the sin of omission described by this verse seems at first sight disconnected from the topic of planning for the future, the word **'then'** ('therefore', RSV) associates it firmly with what has gone before. If this is so, then **'the good'** we ought to do is to plan for the future humbly, acknowledging that life is uncertain, we are transient and God is sovereign. This is the natural way of understanding what seems to be a proverbial saying that James has borrowed and inserted into his letter (notice the way he changes from the second-person 'you' in the previous verses to the third-person 'he'). To fail to do what we know is right when we plan for the future is the sin described as boasting and bragging (4:16). This is a recurrent theme of being not just a hearer, but also a doer of the word. Pride is not only an attitude that deliberately ignores God; it is also a failure to practise what we know to be right (see Luke 12:47-48).

## Conclusion

In the light of this passage the kinds of questions we should be asking ourselves before we commence a new venture would be something like this:

- Do I genuinely desire to bring the whole of my life under his lordship?
- Are my plans wholly God-honouring, or are they selfishly motivated?
- Are the means of achieving them good and proper?
- Have I made them a matter of prayer from the outset?
- Would I be content should God say 'No'?

- Would I be prepared to admit that perhaps my plans were wrong?
- Am I willing to submit to his will should my plans fail?

We know we should trust God in our planning, but do we? Are we afraid that he might not agree with our plans? Is there a member of the opposite sex with whom we really want to develop a relationship, but we are afraid the Lord might say 'No' if we submit the plan to him (perhaps because the person is not yet a Christian)? Are we trying to manipulate circumstances so that our plans work out? Can we really bring the Lord into this or that activity? Fearing his disapproval, do we neglect to make it a matter of prayer?

# 21.
# When is much too much?



I live in a society which loves to consume, and does so with abandon. We have become preoccupied with real estate, renovations, interest rates, credit cards and tax cuts. There is unprecedented affluence, but at the same time personal debt is increasing. The human toll is more difficult to quantify. While we are certainly better off, we are not more satisfied. An increasing number of researchers are linking consumerism with unhappiness, symptoms of which range from obesity to depression. Riches are no guarantee of a happier life.

First of all, we need to acknowledge that wealth is a good and generous gift of God (1:17). Churches, missionary societies, Christian aid organizations, as well as individual servants of God, have been the recipients of the generosity of those with wealth. Yet, if we were to try to maintain the balance of Scripture, we would have to concede that riches are spoken of largely in negative terms and that wealth can corrupt even the best of men and women. The parable of the sower warns of 'the deceitfulness of wealth' (Matt. 13:22). Jesus taught his disciples that it would be hard for a rich man to enter the kingdom of heaven (Matt. 19:23). Paul wrote to his junior co-worker Timothy warning that the love of money is *a* (not *the*, as in some translations) root of all kinds of evil (1 Tim. 6:10).

James again addresses the wealthy and writes, **'Now listen, you rich people, weep and wail because of the misery that is coming upon you.'** But who are the rich people whom James has in mind? (See also the discussion on 1:9-12.) Some have linked them with the wealthy entrepreneurs in the previous section (4:13-16). Like them, those in view here fail to acknowledge a sovereign God over the whole of life, but the resemblance ends there. These rich people are not believers, because James nowhere calls them **'brothers'** — his usual and affectionate term for fellow Christians. In fact he speaks of them in terms of condemnation and of the terrible punishments that await them.

**What is the fault of these rich people?**

*1. They 'have hoarded wealth in the last days' (5:3)*

'Hoarding' conveys the idea of accumulation of more than is needed. This does not mean we should cash in our superannuation or not put by for a 'rainy day'. The Old Testament comments favourably on the ant who stores up in summer for what is needed in winter (Prov. 6:6-8). Each believer is to work in order to provide for his family, because not to do so is to behave worse than an unbeliever (1 Tim. 5:8). Rather, the accumulation of possessions in a selfish manner betrays a person who views life solely in material terms.

*2. They have 'failed to pay' the wages of their employees (5:4)*

Perhaps they might have defended themselves as being too busy or blamed their failure to pay on the market. The reality was that they withheld wages while they were making large profits themselves. I am reminded of company executives rewarding themselves with huge salary increases while wage rises for employees are kept pitifully low.

## 3. Their 'self-indulgence' (5:5)

The equivalent today is the world of high-end real estate, the latest model luxury car, gourmet eating, holidays in fashionable places and an extravagant lifestyle. James bluntly calls it what it is — extravagance and self-indulgence.

## 4. They are oppressive (5:6)

**'You have condemned and murdered innocent men, who were not opposing you.'** Today the rich do not usually resort to physical violence against those who stand in their way, but may find other measures to achieve their goals. The legal system can be manipulated to protect selfish interests. The poor simply do not have the means to sustain a long and protracted court battle; the cost of litigation is prohibitive. Although I live in a country with a healthy constitution and legal system, it has still not been strong enough to prevent a growing number of scandals that have left what Australians call 'the battler' (i.e. the little man) impoverished. Only a relatively robust economy has been able to support the cost of corruption by some company executives — a luxury many countries do not enjoy.

## Why is it foolish?

James selects three characteristic marks of worldly riches — namely *wealth* (probably a reference to the harvest from their fields), *clothing* and *precious metals*. Their wealth **'has

**rotted'** — if by 'wealth' is meant the produce of harvest, this is a reference to mildew or vermin. Clothing is open to insect attack (**'moths'**) and precious metals to corrosion.

Earthly treasure, no matter how well guarded, can be lost through inflation, a stock-market crash, theft, recession, fire, political upheaval, or breakage. By contrast, Peter writes of the believer's true wealth, which is 'an inheritance that can never perish, spoil or fade — kept in heaven for you' (1 Peter 1:4).

Christian young people can have a wonderful idealism about wealth. At twenty years of age it is relatively easy to be free from the love of riches. James reminds us to take care not to lose that idealism, to be careful when financial pressures increase and when opportunities for career advancement or promotion come. All too often the cutting edge of Christian testimony is blunted by daily interaction with the world. Success, if it comes, brings with it material gain, but it can also be accompanied by a growing lukewarmness to the gospel. Far too many who began well in their youth can no longer say, 'For to me, to live is Christ and to die is gain' (Phil. 1:21). There is a constant battle to be waged, one for which vigilance is required. We are to be on guard lest we become possessed by our possessions.

**How will they fare?**

James rebukes this wealthy group of landowners: **'Weep and wail because of the misery that is coming upon you'** (5:1). The selfish heaping up of wealth will **'testify against'** them (5:3) that they have put their trust in material things. The statement that it **'will eat your flesh like fire'** indicates the torment of a conscience consumed by guilt and regret in the fires of hell. **'You have fattened yourselves in the day of slaughter'** (5:5) points forward to the day when the Lord will bring the whole of mankind into judgement. These wealthy men are likened to cattle destined for the abattoir, unaware that they are being fed for slaughter. Those whom they have defrauded cry out for justice and their prayer reaches **'the ears of the Lord Almighty'**. The vivid imagery parallels the way in which the blood of Abel cried out to God from the ground for vindication (Gen. 4:10).

The outcome of a life lived for selfish gain is misery. In one sense that misery is partly experienced in this life. Yet in another sense the full weight of God's wrath is reserved for the future. Jesus spoke of God's wrath on several occasions. He went about doing good — giving sight to the blind, healing the sick, casting out demons, raising the dead and speaking with divine wisdom and grace. He preached the gospel to the poor, and by his death on the cross offers pardon and life to all who repent. Yet he also warned of the possibility of a final rejection by God and the terrors of hell to follow.

It would be easy to read a section like this one and feel somewhat smug that there are sins mentioned here that we may never have the opportunity to commit. But we don't need to be rich to be covetous, nor do we need to be wealthy to be selfish. The seeds of these things lie within us all and are just itching to break out. A passage like this warns us of danger, directs us to make changes where necessary and points us to Christ and his grace for cleansing and pardon.

The whole passage is reminiscent of the way the Old Testament prophets pronounced doom upon those who misused their riches and power. They warned those who paid unfair wages, who defrauded their workers, who got rich at the expense of the poor and who denied them justice (e.g. Amos 5:11-12; Mal. 3:5). Poverty is still a pressing reality in our world, with one in five (and two thirds of them women) living in destitution, as well as extreme inequalities between rich and poor. In this situation we have a responsibility to work in order that we might have something to share with those in need. When we have something to share we are to do so willingly and generously (Eph. 4:28; 1 Tim. 6:17-18). The Old Testament prophets considered the poor not simply as objects of charity who needed relief, but as victims of powerful and often affluent people who abused their positions. The wealthy may seek to lay the blame on the poor for their condition, but Christians are called to champion their cause and to work for remedies at an individual and community level. We do so because we seek to imitate God, who has a special regard for the poor (2:5).

# 22.
# Waiting patiently until the coming of the Lord

*Please read James 5:7-11*

*I waited for the Lord my God,*
*and patiently did bear;*
*At length to me he did incline*
*my voice and cry to hear*
(Ps. 40:1, *The Scottish Psalter*, 1929).

Technology has given us access to so many of the things we desire without the need to wait: if we are hungry, microwavable meals; if we need to contact someone, mobile phones; if we want entertainment, a push of the TV remote control. And, of course, there is no need to save up for what we want when a credit card allows immediate purchase. We have become used to instant gratification. Patience is not a popular virtue today. A wall poster in the study of a minister friend captures the prevailing mood: 'Lord, give me patience and give it to me now!'

Unlike the previous section, which dealt with the un-believer, James signals a return to his readership by again addressing them as **'brothers'**. Patience is the theme of verses 7-11. James begins by commanding it: **'Be patient, then, brothers, until the Lord's coming.'** He then uses the word a further three times, together with the related words

**'persevered'** and **'perseverance'** (5:11). The letter is coming full circle. The testing of our faith by trials, which produces perseverance and leads to maturity, lies at its very heart (1:2-4). James comes back to perseverance now and enlarges on the kind we need.

The connecting word **'then'** ('therefore', RSV) in verse 7 is a clue to why patience was needed by James' readers. They were facing oppression at the hands of the ungodly rich (5:4-6). Yet we cannot restrict James' teaching about the need for patience solely to this context. Job is cited as an example of perseverance, and his trials do not fit into that category (5:11). Also James is writing to Christians who faced various kinds of trials (1:2). Patience is required in every trial because our trust in God's love is put to the test. There are many circumstances in life beyond our control; there are people we cannot change and unjust decisions over which we have no say, as well as decisions we have made and now regret. The temptation might be to get angry (4:1), or complain (5:9), but James leaves us in no doubt about what our basic attitude is to be — patience until the Lord's coming.

However, this patience is no ordinary attitude of calmness. The person who is not a Christian has no access to this kind of patience. It is spiritual, and only the children of God possess it, because only they love the Lord and look for his coming. The unbeliever is not comforted by the thought of the coming of the Lord. Instead natural courage, political ideals or social justice may sustain him. Commendable as these might be, they are the stuff of this world and temporal by nature. Godly patience, on the other hand, is distinguished from natural patience because it has an eschatological (i.e. future) focus and foundation.

If we are among those who look forward to the return of the Lord and do not find our strength and drive from worldly sources, we shall be able to cope with trials. If we would willingly exchange worldly attainment, comforts, pleasures and successes for the near presence of our glorious Jesus Christ, then no adversity can cause our faith to waver. The people of Israel were not sorry to reach Canaan's borders after forty years of wandering in the wilderness. Canaan was the goal of their journey, their earthly inheritance promised by God. No tears were shed then for all the privations and difficulties of wilderness living. So it is too, in a far more glorious way, for the believer. His patience is formed from, and sustained by, a look to the return of the one who has redeemed him from sin, guilt and separation from all that is good and pure. The believer looks forward to his heavenly Canaan when Christ comes to make all things new.

Final vindication and relief from oppression are not promised in this life. The patience James enjoins spans our entire life or until Christ returns, whichever is sooner. This is the death knell to all 'health and wealth' teaching. Nowhere in the Bible are we promised freedom from suffering and an easy ride home. The way to life is narrow and the path hard (cf. 1 Peter 5:10).

## An illustration of waiting patiently (5:7-8)

In another example from the natural world, James notes that the farmer has to wait patiently **'for the autumn and spring rains'** (cf. Deut. 11:14). Both were needed to ensure a good harvest. The coming of the rains is an event the farmer must wait and look to God for (cf. Jer. 5:24; Joel 2:23).

James also encourages us to **'stand firm'** (5:8). We hold firm by actively demonstrating our faith when in contrary circumstances. Patience is not a passive determination to stand fast in the face of the storm, but to make progress by it. A yacht can ride out a gale with a strong anchor, or it can set the sails, taking advantage of the wind to bring it closer to its destination.

The need to establish our hearts is **'because the Lord's coming is near'** (5:8). The nearness is not one of simple time, since no one knows the day or the hour of the Lord's return (Matt. 24:36; Acts 1:7). So we do not scan the future horizon, like the prophets of old, enquiring about the nature and time of his coming (1 Peter 1:10-11). The nearness is rather that of sequence. The next event in the Bible's calendar of redemptive history is Christ's coming. By his incarnation Old Testament prophecies were fulfilled. With his death and resurrection the last days were inaugurated. One event yet remains which is scheduled to usher in the climax of our salvation, and that is the 'Parousia', or Christ's return in glory (Matt. 24:37; 2 Thess. 2:8). This nearness (for it could be at any time) motivates us to make every effort to grow in maturity and live godly lives.

**Waiting impatiently** (5:9)

Though this verse may appear to be disconnected from the previous one, the two are in fact linked. Grumbling is a mark of impatience and an indication that faith has failed, so that what was meant as a test has become a temptation. Grumbling against others (probably other Christians in this context) is a sin that occurs whenever we lapse into thinking that the world is not fully under God's control. It shows a lack of self-control in the face of provocation, and it is fuelled by feelings of frustration, hurt or anger. Grumbling is an attempt to defend our interests, or to get back at those whom we perceive to have wronged us. But to give in to grumbling is to expose ourselves to condemnation because **'the Judge is standing at the door'** (5:9, cf. Matt. 7:21-23; Acts 17:31).

While the warning against misuse of speech is akin to the one given previously (4:11-12), the additional information that 'the Judge is standing at the door' reminds us not just that judgement is imminent (the previous verse has also told us that the coming of the Lord is near), but that believers are subject to scrutiny in the coming judgement, and that assessment of our 'works' will lead to reward for wise stewardship, or loss where we have been unfaithful (cf. 1 Cor. 3:10-15).

## The reward of waiting patiently (5:10-11)

In both the examples of trials that follow (the prophets and Job) we are reminded of the blessedness of those who persevere (cf. 1:12).

The first example is that of the prophets who, in the face of suffering, were patient. Jesus also spoke of them in a similar way (Matt. 5:11-12; 23:29-36). Suffering was the normal experience of God's spokesmen in the Bible. Stephen, as he defended his preaching of Jesus as the Christ, challenged the high priest to name one prophet who was not persecuted (Acts 7:52). Although James does not single out any one prophet by name, we can think of the sufferings of Jeremiah or Isaiah.

The other example is Job, who suffered the loss of his wealth, livelihood, children and health in a series of 'accidents'. Unbeknown to him, these losses were the result of a transaction in heaven. Satan doubted Job's integrity, accusing him of fearing God for selfish advantage rather than from a pure love: 'Does Job fear God for nothing?' (Job 1:9). God granted Satan limited power to cause suffering and to test Job's faith. Job's friends who came to comfort him cast doubt on his innocence and thus increased his mental anguish. They concluded that he must have done something wrong to deserve this kind of calamity at the hand of God.

James mentions **'Job's perseverance'**. Under severe trial he 'did not sin by charging God with wrongdoing' (Job 1:22) and, even when provoked by his wife to 'curse God and die', he was unyielding in defending the goodness of God (Job 2:9,10). James' readers are then invited to reflect upon **'what the Lord finally brought about'** in Job's life, which was the result of the trials he endured — namely what is set out in the closing section of the book (Job 38 – 42). At the conclusion of that book we discover that Job's fortunes were restored, that he raised another family and that the Lord blessed his latter days more than his former ones. But we must not think that the reversal in Job's fortunes was a reward for passing the test of faith.

More importantly, we find an encounter in which the Lord revealed himself to Job in a new way. What the Lord brought about for Job was a deeper knowledge of himself. In particular Job came to appreciate that **'the Lord is full of compassion and mercy'** (5:11). Job still didn't know the reason for his suffering. He knew nothing of the transaction between God and Satan. But he did know that God knew the reason for his trials and he was happy to rest his faith in that knowledge. Above all, he knew that God is compassionate and not capricious. He does not willingly afflict the sons of men. Job also learnt that when God withdraws his temporal blessings and leads us through dark waters, we can know the full measure of his mercy in fresh ways. Derek Thomas comments:

> As we have already seen, there had been a time when Job failed to imagine God ever being good to him again or any renewal of his own life. Everything that was dear to him was taken away. There remained only the certainty of death. God's pruning shears had

seemed devoid of mercy and, like the tree which had been cut down, there was no hope for him.

But spring came again to Job's life. It was spring of such beauty and fragrance that the bitterness of the past seemed almost forgotten. Hope and life and joy returned in abundance. In God's way of doing things, winter is followed by springtime. For some it may be in just the very terms given to Job. But for others, the blessing will be even greater. It will not be a blessing of life in this world but a fuller and better life in the world to come.[1]

There is an elderly believer I know who is suffering the effects of age and ill-health. When I ask, 'How are you?' he replies, 'Nothing that a good resurrection will not cure'! Those trials in the present, which may strip away many of the God-given comforts and achievements enjoyed in the past, compel us to look to the future with renewed patience and eager hope. The believer is sustained by the knowledge that his or her present trials find their ultimate meaning in the Lord Jesus Christ, who has suffered patiently for us and for our salvation and who is the coming Lord. His goal for us is that we should grow in grace, develop a truly Christlike character and deepen our knowledge and love of him (cf. 1:2-4). As such we must always hold lightly the things of this world and set our hope fully on 'the grace to be given you when Jesus Christ is revealed' (1 Peter 1:13).

# 23.
# Do not swear

*Please read James 5:12*

The word 'swear' is usually understood today as meaning to use bad language. So when we read, 'Do not swear', we might think in terms of crude or obscene language. All too often (even in Christian circles) we hear language that vents frustration or surprise, often using the name of God or Christ, as well as a range of expressions that, while not specifically religious, are nevertheless repugnant. This kind of swearing is referred to by Paul in his letter to the Ephesians. He writes that we should not engage in talk that involves filthiness or coarse joking. Rather, our speech is to be spiced with the acknowledgement of God's goodness, and edifying to those who hear (Eph. 5:1-6).

However, when James writes, **'Do not swear'**, he means calling on some greater power to bear witness that our word is true, or our promise credible, in order to convince others. Sometimes that involves the name of God directly, but not always. The Jewish believers to whom James wrote were swearing by **'heaven'** (a euphemism for God) and by **'earth'** (to stress the truth of their word) and also using other un-specified oaths (5:12).

Every time we make a promise our personal integrity is at stake. By swearing an oath we are creating a new category of truth which is supposedly more reliable. James will have none of these double standards. Rather, we are to say what we mean and mean what we say.

There is a strong parallel between James' teaching and that of Jesus in the Sermon on the Mount. Setting the two passages alongside each other helps to show the similarities:

| *James 5:12* | *Matthew 5:34-37* |
|---|---|
| Above all, my brothers, | But I tell you, |
| do not swear — | Do not swear at all: |
| not by heaven | either by heaven, for it is God's throne; |
| or by earth | or by the earth, for it is his footstool; |
| or by anything else. | or by Jerusalem … [or] by your head… |
| Let your 'Yes,' be yes, | Simply let your 'Yes' be 'Yes', |
| and your 'No', no, | and your 'No', 'No'; |
| or you will be condemned. | anything beyond this comes from the evil one. |

James is drawing on a well-established saying of Jesus, who is in turn responding to a wrong interpretation by the rabbis of Old Testament law. We need to go back first of all to the law, to discover where this teaching originated, then to consider our Lord's correction of rabbinic interpretation and finally to come back to what James teaches and apply his words to ourselves.

## What the law says

The background to this teaching on swearing is found in the Old Testament, where permission is given to swear an oath, even oaths using the name of God. The Third Commandment is one of a number of passages that permit swearing an oath (Exod. 20:7). It does not prohibit swearing, but rather false swearing. The commandment is often mistakenly thought to forbid bad language or blasphemy. However, it is concerned with a more serious matter — the misuse of God's name. In a further expansion of this basic command Moses also permitted swearing. He wrote that 'When a man makes a vow to the LORD, or takes an oath to bind himself by a pledge, he must not break his word but must do everything he said' (Num. 30:2). And again, 'Fear the LORD your God and serve him. Hold fast to him and take your oaths in his name' (Deut. 10:20). In fact a survey of the Old Testament reveals that the practice was fairly common. Abraham, Jacob, the judges, the kings, as well as the people of Israel, all made a practice of swearing oaths.

Is it then the case that the Old Testament permits what the New Testament forbids? Not at all. Even in the New Testament we find the same pattern. Paul, for example, invokes God's name when he calls on God as witness to the truth of something he has said or done. In the context of Paul's troubled relations with the Corinthian church he says, 'I call God as my witness that it was in order to spare you that I did not return to Corinth' (2 Cor. 1:23). This is no isolated example (cf. Rom. 1:9; Gal. 1:20; Phil. 1:8; 1 Thess. 2:5,10).

The swearing of an oath is designed to underline the solemn nature of the promises we make. Even God himself uses oaths to confirm what he has said. However, this is a gracious condescension to our unbelief rather than any need on his part to underline the truth of what he promises (e.g. Heb. 6:13-18).

## What Jesus taught (Matt. 5:34-37)

If swearing was permitted in the law, why do Jesus and James say, 'Do not swear'? The answer lies in the observation that Jesus was not responding to the law as such, but to a wrong interpretation of it. The rabbis taught: 'Do not break your oath, but keep the oaths you have made to the Lord' (Matt. 5:33). While that might seem to reflect the law, it was in fact a perversion of it. The rabbis focused on the *wording* of the oath rather than on its *intent*. The *intention* of the law from the beginning was telling the truth; however, the rabbis made distinctions between oaths, depending on how they were *worded*. Some were binding; others were not. For example, to swear on the temple was not binding, but to swear on the gold of the temple was (Matt. 23:16-22). Jesus taught that these distinctions of wording were not only irrelevant; they revealed something worse — double standards relating to speech. If we promise something, we must keep our word whether or not we swore to it.

We are now in a better position to understand the injunction not to swear. In context it is not a blanket prohibition against swearing. Rather it is a recognition that the tongue is a 'restless evil, full of deadly poison' (3:8). In a world where dishonesty is commonplace, the act of swearing is something that is permitted, not a command of the law. It is a concession to the sinfulness of man. Just as divorce is unpalatable but allowed in the Scripture (under certain conditions) due to the hardness of man's heart, so too is oath-taking. However, the Christian transformed by grace is called to integrity of speech. We are to say what we mean and to keep our word. If everyone told the truth all the time there would be no need for swearing. It is a poor theology that takes the command of Jesus and of James in an absolute sense without sensitivity to the context.

**What James adds** (5:12)

James, in restating the command of Jesus, introduces it with the phrase **'above all'**. By this he is not intending that the prohibition on swearing is the most important thing in the whole letter (it would not be more important, for example, than 'the royal law'); rather, he is starting to bring his letter to a conclusion. Where Paul says 'finally' (Phil. 3:1; 4:8; 1 Thess. 4:1; 2 Thess. 3:1), James says 'above all'. After everything that James has said about the tongue, he signals that he is coming back for the last time to a key topic of the letter.

The connection to what has gone before and what comes after is not easily discerned. If we look backwards perhaps swearing is a sign of impatience (5:7), or perhaps the link is with the coming of the Lord as future Judge (5:8-9), in the light of which we need to guard the integrity of what we say. If the link is with what follows, then the context is prayer (5:13-18). When we invoke God's name (as we do in prayer) we are to guard against misusing it by empty words.

James is passionately concerned for integrity of speech. As the people of God, we claim to have the truth (or perhaps it is more accurate to say, the truth has us). We follow the one who calls himself 'the way and the truth and the life' (John 14:6). What better witness than when our words show a transparent commitment to truth? In practice this will mean avoiding as much as possible the practice of swearing. As we progress into the maturity that James desires we shall become known as men and women of integrity — our 'Yes' will mean yes and our 'No' will mean no.

## What this passage has to say to us today

While we do not know the exact nature of the swearing which prompted James to caution against it, none the less his injunction may be applied to three areas of the Christian life.

### 1. The command promotes the honour of God

At the heart of this command lies a burning passion for the honour of God. Swearing in a first-century Jewish situation was invariably made in a religious context. God's name was invoked and he was called to witness the statement made, or the promise given. However, since the Jews had an aversion to using the name of God, some had developed a sophisticated casuistry for swearing oaths and thus avoided the intent of the law. James provides a couple of common examples (**'by heaven'** and **'by earth'**), but the practice was clearly not restricted to these (**'or anything else'**).

*Coram Deo* is a phrase which means 'in the presence of God' and is used in Christian theology to express the idea that we live (and speak) at all times in his presence, under his authority and for his glory. To depart from this passage thinking, 'I must be more careful what I say or swear', misses the point. It is to mistake the symptom for the cause. The injunction primarily calls us to a renewed reverence for God. The more that we reflect on his name and honour, the more we shall find our delight and satisfaction in being truthful for him. Irreverence towards God goes together with carelessness of speech. On the other hand, telling the truth becomes a habit when we realize that we are always in his presence and that he is the silent hearer of every conversation. The extent to which we are passionate for his name will be proportional to the concern we show to let our 'Yes' be yes and our 'No' be no.

## 2. The command advances integrity of speech

The intent of this command is that we become less interested in swearing oaths and more concerned with telling the truth. Swearing to tell the truth, no matter what its form might take and while it is required in some circumstances, always brings what a person says under suspicion. When the word of a person is under scrutiny, such as in a court of law, swearing may be necessary, but at the same time it is an admission of human frailty and sinfulness. Sometimes a plain 'Yes' or 'No' is not enough.

For the rest of the time, however, we are to aim for personal integrity by straightforward speaking. Better to declare a simple 'Yes' or 'No' than to strengthen our speech with meaningless phrases. Thus, for example, the person who frequently says, 'To be quite honest with you …', may not be quite so honest with you — at least not all the time. And the person who says, 'To tell you the truth …' may not have been telling you all the truth you needed to hear. Have we got into the habit when making promises of adding words or phrases to reinforce the truth of what we say to others — 'I really will do it', 'honest, I will', 'cross my heart and hope to die' and 'so help me' — rather than simply saying, 'I will do it'? Communication has become muddled because 'truth' has been distinguished from 'true truth'. This kind of speaking masks reality with soothing phrases which reassure the hearer but introduce higher degrees of truth.

Integrity of speech is essential to community. Without it trust is lost and relationships break down. To churches which show all the symptoms of infighting and disunity, James' command is necessary and to the point. The tongue is especially unruly in disagreements with others. We are tempted to gain the advantage in arguments by exaggeration with statements such as, 'You *never* learn,' or 'You *always* forget,' or 'You do that *every* time.' Have we become accustomed to strengthening our speech in this manner?

The more we are known for integrity of speech, the more we adorn the gospel. If we can be trusted in what we say on mundane matters, then people may be more inclined to listen to us on spiritual ones. May our words be used to commend the gospel of our glorious Lord Jesus Christ openly, clearly and accurately!

### 3. The command warns of condemnation

While Jesus warns of the demonic origins of false oaths (Matt. 5:37), James warns of their outcome: '**... you will be condemned.**' The thought here is connected to that of the earlier verses which warned of the threat of an imminent verdict — 'The judge is standing at the door'.

What a high value God places on our words! We might treat them casually, or forget what we say, but he doesn't. If we say, 'Oh! I didn't intend it to be taken that seriously,' the fact of the matter is that God does and will hold us account-able on the Day of Judgement for 'every careless word' (Matt. 12:36). Why God should put such a premium on our words is not stated, but it surely has to do with the integrity of his word, which reveals the absolute trustworthiness of his character.

> Who may ascend the hill of the LORD?
>> Who may stand in his holy place?
> He who has clean hands and a pure heart,
>> who does not lift up his soul to an idol
>> *or swear by what is false*
>>>> (Ps. 24:3-4, italics added).

# 24.
# A prayer for all seasons

*Please read James 5:13-18*

**When to pray** (5:13)

The opening verse of this section reminds us that life is not a monotonous, bland affair (5:13). There are seasons to life — ups and downs, joys and sorrows, the *annus horribilis* as well as the *annus mirabilis*[1] (see also Eccles. 3:1-8). Yet there is one constant throughout this changing landscape. It is a God who has loved us in Christ and who gives only good gifts to his children (1:17). When in trouble we are to seek him in prayer. When we are blessed we are not to forget him, but to respond in songs of praise, acknowledging that God is sovereign and graciously invites us to draw near at all times and in all seasons.

**How to pray** (5:14-16)

Praying for the sick is a critical issue today because of the variety of new approaches to healing. Many of these lie outside the bounds of traditional medicine and go hand-in-hand with an unbiblical philosophy. Their practitioners claim special powers that cannot be studied by conventional scientific method. Are they consistent with the Christian faith? Some clearly are not. The sheer variety of alternative therapies is potentially confusing and requires a fresh examination of our approach to healing.

There are many wonderful stories in the Gospels of Jesus dealing with the seriously ill, but they tell us what happened rather than what to do in similar circumstances. The significance of this passage is that it is the only place in the New Testament that is prescriptive, rather than descriptive, in the matter of healing. James sets out a sequence of steps to be followed for those who are sick.

We might add that, even though the principle set out in these verses is prescriptive, it is not restrictive. It does not need to be employed in every case. Other passages in the New Testament suggest the use of ordinary medical means. Jesus mentions the usefulness of a doctor (Mark 2:17); Paul instructs Timothy not to take just water but a little wine for his frequent stomach ailments (1 Tim. 5:23); Trophimus is left by Paul at Miletus (2 Tim. 4:20); and Paul prayed for personal healing from the Lord (2 Cor. 12:7-9) — i.e. he did not call in elders.

Some argue that healing is in the atonement (cf. Isa. 53:5) and therefore no Christian need be sick. But James speaks of **'any one of you'** being sick (5:14). While it is true that healing is in the atonement, not everything in the atonement is the present possession of the Christian. We haven't yet received our resurrection bodies, for example. One of the reasons Jesus healed the sick and raised the dead was a sign that the new age had begun. There will be a new heaven and earth in which all sin, evil, suffering, sickness and death will be eradicated. But that is in the future, when he comes a second time to consummate his kingdom. Indeed, most of the blessings of the kingdom are future. We do receive some blessings now — pardon, forgiveness of sin, reconciliation and the gift of the Holy Spirit. These are blessings won for us at Calvary. However, the time when there will be no more sickness is future, part of the 'not yet'. Nevertheless the passage here encourages us to seek divine healing *now* as an encouragement to faith and hope.

The reference to the sick person suggests someone who is seriously ill (5:14). This is not a course of action for an occasional headache (take a painkiller, or, if the pain persists, see a doctor!), or toothache (see the dentist!). The fact that the elders are called in to visit and **'to pray over him'** and the phrase **'the Lord will raise him up'** suggest a bedridden person. Notice too that the onus is on the sick person to initiate the action. This is a permitted procedure, not a necessity. Although all Christians may pray for healing, James singles out the elders of the church for this ministry. They are mature in the faith and gifted for leadership, and so are naturally the first to be called upon.

The anointing with oil (5:14) could be medicinal, except that oil is not a remedy for every kind of illness. It could be an aid to faith, as when Jesus put mud on the eyes of the man blind from birth (John 9:6). It is certainly not a sacrament (as in the practice of extreme unction). The emphasis is on the prayer, not the oil. Since oil is used in the rest of Scripture to signify the setting apart of a person for special service, the most likely meaning of the oil is the singling out of the sick person to be the object of God's particular care and attention (cf. Exod. 28:41; Acts 4:27).

**'The prayer offered in faith'** is not some higher form of prayer (5:15). No special kind of faith is needed here. The general teaching of Scripture is that all prayer must be offered in faith (cf 1:6). There are no techniques or secrets to extract from God something he has not purposed to do. Faith to remove mountains will avail nothing if it is not according to God's will. Even so, the principle set out in James 5 is given to encourage us to pray for healing, to assure us of

God's concern and to give us confidence to expect divine healing.

The **'if'** in **'if he has sinned'** does not imply the possibility of sinless perfection. Rather, it is included because there may be a link between the sickness and the sin. Sickness in general can be linked to the fall of man into sin (Gen. 3), but not all cases of sickness are the direct result of sin, as Job's friends and the disciples (John 9:2) wrongly thought. Some sicknesses are attributable to the Evil One (Job 2:7; Luke 13:16); others are part of living in a fallen world (1 Tim. 5:23); still others are attributable to a person's sin (Num. 12:9-15; Mark 2:1-12; John 5:14). In the latter case repentance from sin results in divine forgiveness: **'... he will be forgiven.'** The necessary inference is that healing occurs in cases (not all) where sin is the cause of the sickness, or where healing has been hindered by sin. However, the conditional nature of this verse, 'if he has sinned', makes it clear that James does not believe that an individual's sickness is always the result of a sin that he or she has committed.

Confession of sin, which is tightly linked to the repentance described above, together with prayer, is commended to all: **'Therefore confess your sins to each other and pray for each other'** (5:16). No longer are the elders or the seriously sick individual particularly in mind; this is the right and responsibility of every church member. The present tense of the imperative verbs **'confess'** and **'pray'** suggests an ongoing process, making confession and prayer a powerful combination for the general health and well-being of the congregation.

The command to **'confess your sins to each other'** (5:16) does need some further comment. The practice of confession can be, and has been, misused. Cults, or abusive church leaders, can use it as a means of control — to encourage psychological dependency on the leadership, or in other cases to bring followers into line. It can encourage a self-righteous curiosity into the weaknesses of others. Real confession, however, is to be voluntary, confidential, Godward and prayerful. Confession is for the purpose of putting things right with God because sin hinders prayer (Ps. 66:18; Isa. 59:1-2). Wiersbe wisely says that 'We must never confess sin beyond the circle of that sin's influence.' Private sin requires private confession.

**Why we are to pray** (5:16-18)

The way prayer is spoken of in Christian circles sometimes conveys the impression that it is distinct and separable from God. It is as if prayer has some potency in and of itself. For example, we talk about the 'power of prayer', or the 'secret of prayer', and so on. The focus shifts from the one to whom prayer is addressed (God) to the instrument (the act of prayer itself), and we may begin to believe that prayer has some inherent potency and that through it we can get from God what we want. Let us never forget that prayer is nothing but the outworking of a relationship.

The reason why we are to pray is that **'The prayer of a righteous man is powerful and effective'** (5:16). And, for prayer to be anything, there must be a relationship with God that is characterized by what James calls 'righteousness'. God does not obligate himself to people of power, influence, eloquence or wealth. Equally he doesn't commit himself to work through the poor, dreary, unlearned or uninspiring. But he will use *any* kind of person who is righteous, whatever accomplishments he or she may, or may not, have.

The word **'righteous'** has an objective quality to it as well as a subjective meaning. In Romans Paul uses it to describe the objective gift of righteousness given by faith to all who believe. And so the word could simply stand for a believer — he or she is righteous by faith; otherwise the person would not be a Christian. However, given the context of James and the use elsewhere in his letter of the language of 'righteousness', it is more likely that James uses the word in a subjective sense. 'He who does what is right is righteous,' says John (1 John 3:7) and James would add his amen to that as one of the key themes of his letter. In order to pray powerfully it is not just necessary to *be* right with God but to *do* right with God. That is not at all to imply perfection (as the following example of Elijah shows). But we cannot divide effective prayer from righteous conduct, any more than we can divide faith from works. This is another example of that pervasive theme of James applied here in the realm of prayer.

We are told three things about Elijah as an example of prayer.

## 1. He was 'a man just like us' (5:17)

We love to have our heroes. In Christian circles we tend to eulogize the great men and women of the church and to think that by putting them on a pedestal we are released from the responsibility of emulating them: 'They are different'; 'I am not like them.' That may be our excuse, but James will have none of it. Elijah was no superhero; he was **'a man just like us'**.

## 2. The earnestness of Elijah's prayer (5:17)

The literal translation would be: 'He prayed in prayer.' The doubling of the word draws attention to its fervency. The occasion is the prayer for drought and the subsequent prayer for rain during the time of King Ahab in ninth-century Israel. Concerning the former occasion, we can only draw inferences, but of the latter we know much more (1 Kings 18). Elijah prayed seven times. Six times nothing happened; then on the seventh occasion when he sent his servant the latter saw a little cloud like a man's hand rising from the sea. Elijah rushed off in haste to Jezreel after sending a message to the king urging him to set off before his chariot wheels got bogged down in the torrent of rain and mud. The earnestness of his prayer has little to do with passion, or posture, or the length of the prayer. It has everything to do with God's promise of rain (1 Kings 18:1). Elijah knew beforehand that God would answer. Earnestness in prayer flows out of a confidence in the promises of God. Charles Spurgeon wrote, 'Every promise of Scripture is a writing of God which may be pleaded before him with this reasonable request: "Do as you have said."'

### 3. The power of believing prayer

Elijah was a man who prayed to God about climate change. There may be climactic changes needed in our personal and church life. We have the resources to make those changes. In the light of this passage, however, it may not be accurate to speak of the power of prayer; it is better to think of the power of God, who graciously condescends to use our prayer to make the changes he desires.

So we should turn to God in all situations, and James encourages a very sick person to call the leaders of the church for special attention. Faith, anointing with oil, accompanied by prayer (and if appropriate, confession) are to be a part of this service. Elijah is recommended both as an encouragement and an example of the type of prayer needed for divine healing.

# 25.
# The leaver-sensitive church



*Please read James 5:19-20*

Some years ago I attended an isolated church in the Isle of Skye off the west coast of Scotland. Towards the end of the service the minister suddenly announced, 'We will now continue no longer,' at which point the entire congregation stood up and immediately left. It was such an abrupt closure that I and my companions were left alone in the church. By the time we got to the door most of the congregation were disappearing down the glen towards home. James, too, ends in an unexpectedly abrupt manner. There is no benediction. There are no farewell greetings, just an exhortation to recover those who stray from the gospel.

His final word is typical of his pastoral approach. The address, **'my brothers'**, is followed by an appeal to show a responsibility and concern for other brothers who are straying from the faith and perhaps may have left the church. James has written some hard things in his letter. He has occasionally used some strong words; he has had much to say about the faults and weaknesses of the churches of the diaspora. Nevertheless, he is passionately concerned for the unity and maturity of the believers to whom he is writing. He still believes in the 'holy, catholic church'. Despite its many failures, it is still the church which Christ loves and for whom Christ died. What a challenge to us as well! It is all too easy to become disenchanted and cynical about the church, or individuals in it. Do we share James' passion and commitment to the beloved brothers?

## A condition to escape (5:19)

In recent years much thought has been given to making the church more welcoming to those on the outside. The so-called 'seeker-sensitive' approach places an emphasis on making the church an attractive place to attend. Strategies employed include the presentation of short, anecdotal sermons that address felt needs and avoid the mention of sin, death and judgement, contemporary music that is professionally played, no taking up of offerings, and the provision of community support services such as childcare. While the motive of winning the lost for Christ is commendable, some of the methods used are questionable and have been criticized.

While we may hold to an evangelical faith that seeks to bring the gospel to people without Christ and see them added to the church, do we know what to do with those who leave the faith? Nowhere near the same amount of thought has been given to help pick up the early clues that someone may be going to withdraw from church and abandon the faith. At the end of his letter James is concerned that we develop a sensitivity to such individuals.

Of course, people move away from a church for all kinds of reasons — sometimes with justification, because of moving house, and sometimes for reasons that are less transparent. One of the trends observed by sociologists among the so-called 'Generation X' (those reaching adulthood in the 1980s and 1990s) is of less adherence to doctrinal distinctions or denominations. 'Choice' is the watchword, and many look for a church as they would choose a brand of detergent in the supermarket, shopping around for a church which most suits their particular social needs and with which they feel 'comfortable' (a notoriously slippery word). Consumerism has become a way of life for all of us, which is a regrettable trend when it is applied to choosing the church we attend.

However, that is not the direct concern of the exhortation in verse 19. James is thinking here of those **'who wander from the truth'**, by which he does not mean that they have suddenly become dishonest and prefer to tell lies. Nor does he necessarily mean that they have embraced a version of the gospel which is false. Rather, he has in mind people who have drifted away from their Christian commitment and withdrawn from fellowship with other believers. The reasons may be doctrinal (they no longer hold dear the central truths of the gospel) or behavioural (they no longer desire to live by the standards found in Scripture). Given the frequent references in the letter to the problems caused by wealth (1:9-11; 2:1-7; 4:3,13-15; 5:1-6), James probably has in mind some at least who in their enthusiasm for riches had drifted from the truth. Paul too observed this same trend: 'Some people, eager for money, have wandered from the faith and pierced themselves with many griefs' (1 Tim. 6:10). It is to a wandering brother or sister such as this that James calls our attention.

Notice that the person requiring this ministry is described indefinitely: **'If one of you should wander from the truth...'** This I find quite sobering. Let us not think that we are immune and imagine that it could never happen to us. Sheep are prone to stray. We shall not find any story in the Bible about sheep looking for a straying shepherd. Robert Robinson was converted under the preaching of George Whitefield and in 1758, three years later, wrote the hymn, 'Come, Thou Fount of Every Blessing'. In it he records his own experience of how the heart can drift:

Oh, to grace how great a debtor
Daily I'm constrained to be!
Let thy goodness, like a fetter,
Bind my wand'ring heart to thee;
Prone to wander, Lord, I feel it,
Prone to leave the God I love;
Here's my heart, O take and seal it;
Seal it for thy courts above
                    (Robert Robinson, 1735–1790).

Let him who thinks he stands take heed lest he fall. Believers can be deceived (the word **'wander'** can also mean 'to be deceived' and has already been used in that way by James in 1:16). Robert Robinson did wander in later life, preaching against the full divinity of Christ. There are those too, like Demas, a co-worker of the apostle Paul, active in ministry among the churches (Col. 4:14), who in the end fell in love with the world and deserted his post (2 Tim. 4:10).

During the nineteenth century Octavius Winslow, besides holding several pastorates in England, became a prolific writer of Christian books. One of the books that he wrote, *Personal Declension and Revival in the Soul*, offered godly wisdom to those who had drifted from Christ. He warned of the need for constant vigilance lest, in the busyness of life, one overlooked the cultivation of the soul before God:

If there is one consideration more humbling than another to a spiritually-minded believer, it is, that after all God has done for him — after all the rich displays of his grace, the patience and tenderness of his instructions, the repeated discipline of his covenant, the tokens of his love received, and the lessons of experience learned, there should still exist in the heart a principle, the tendency of which is to secret, perpetual, and alarming departure from God. Truly, there is in this solemn fact, that which might well lead to the deepest self-abasement before him.


## A care to exercise (5:19-20)

The plain fact of the matter is that we have a duty of care to one another. Cain had no regard at all for his brother Abel. In reply to God's question as to the whereabouts of his brother, he retorted, 'Am I my brother's keeper?' (Gen. 4:9). As part of the one family of God, we have a duty and responsibility to each other. And since the appeal is indefinite, '**...and *someone* should bring him back**' (italics added), this is a duty that is shared by us all, and not restricted to the minister, elders or other leaders in the church. We cannot opt out of this ministry piously protesting that the Lord will bring him or her back, or the Holy Spirit will convict the wanderer. Of course, it might be possible that the Lord will directly intervene, but he normally uses secondary causes to accomplish his work, and that means *us*. This is a pastoral ministry assigned to each one of us.

Sometimes those who wander are likely to be those who are wounded or disillusioned. In this situation the ministry of restoration is unlikely to be straightforward. Sensitivity and care will be needed. Without it we may end up creating more damage and a result worse than when we started. Paul gives advice for those engaged in a ministry of recovery. He writes, 'Brothers, if someone is caught in a sin, you who are spiritual should restore him gently. But watch yourself, or you also may be tempted. Carry each other's burdens, and in this way you will fulfil the law of Christ' (Gal. 6:1-2).

Not everyone is suited to bringing back someone caught in a sin. When Paul writes, 'you who are spiritual', he is thinking of the believer who is mature — someone whose life manifests the fruit of the indwelling Holy Spirit. If we do not have a genuine love for the wanderer, this is not the ministry for us. If our lives are not submitted to God's Word and controlled by his Spirit, we should leave the task to others. If we think, 'I can do this,' or 'I'll put this person right,' or 'I know what's wrong with them,' and proceed in the confidence of our own ability, then we are disqualified. A conscious recognition of our own weakness and need of God's wisdom and grace is essential.

Paul also singles out an attitude of gentleness. Of all the fruit of the Spirit this one is identified as essential. The implication is that those caught in a sin are suffering and therefore in a delicate state. We do not want to add further injury by adopting a harsh or self-righteous attitude. We shall need to be able to speak the truth in love and be sensitive to their circumstances. If we don't suffer fools gladly, cannot control our tongues, are slow to hear, quick to speak and easily irritated, then let others do this work.

Finally, we are also to look to ourselves lest we also be tempted. The dangers are great because the heart is quick to feel pleasure in the follies of others. The self-righteous heart of the Pharisee whispers within, 'God, I thank you that I am not like other men' (Luke 18:11). We may pride ourselves on our ability to be wise judges of character and may be very good at identifying the imperfections of others (see Matt. 7:3-5). But place that alongside a natural blindness to our own shortcomings and a tendency to read our own abilities through rose-tinted spectacles, and we have a sure recipe for failure. Only where there is a deep sense of our own unworthiness and prayerful dependency upon God should an attempt at recovery be made. Even then there is no assurance of success. No guarantees are given. Sin has a strong and persistent grip.

## A consequence to esteem (5:20)

However, where recovery is successful the blessings are many. Far from discouraging us, James lays out the good that can be achieved. There are two consequences.

*1. The erring brother is brought back from a pathway that leads to spiritual death*

**'Death'** is the final destination of those who continue unchecked down this road. Here is a reminder of the stark reality of heaven and hell, life and death, being finally joined to Christ or becoming eternally separated from him.

*2. 'A multitude of sins' are covered* (cf. Prov. 10:12; 1 Peter 4:8)

While the language is a little ambiguous, in that it is not clear whose sins are forgiven — those of the restored person or the one who restores — the context almost certainly means the former. It is his sins that have caused him to wander from the truth and it is his salvation that is hoped for by this ministry. James intends that when a person is restored in this way we are to rejoice that he or she has been saved from spiritual ruin and that the person's sins, which were many and grievous, have been pardoned. This glorious ministry points to the power and glory of Christ's saving work on behalf of sinners on the cross of Calvary.

We have now come full circle. The challenge to the church is to become a community showing practical love and care and not focused on ourselves as individuals, or on our own security and comforts. Do we share that sense of pastoral concern? Are we so actively engaged in his service to the extent that we care for the wanderer and desire to grow *together* to maturity? This is another call to let our faith be made visible by works of love.

This final exhortation is consistent with one of the pervasive themes of the letter — namely an appeal for a working faith. Faith in Christ not only saves us from our sin, but also confers upon us the honourable title 'brothers'— and, of course 'sisters'. And if we are brothers, then faith brings with it a duty of care. If a person drifts from gospel belief or behaviour we are to help him or her if we can. If effective we shall be saving that person from spiritual death — the ultimate destiny of those who continue unchecked to wander from Christ.

# Notes

**Introduction**
1. The word 'brother' occurs nineteen times in James. Fifteen of those occurrences are plural and each of these is used to address the scattered believers (1:2,16,19; 2:1,5,14; 3:1,10,12; 4:11; 5:7,9,10,12,19). Statistically the word comes third in importance as a keyword behind 'works' and 'faith'. A keyword in this case is one whose frequency is unusually high in comparison with its use in the rest of the New Testament. Such words can be useful indicators of important themes.
2. J. B. Mayor, *The Epistle of James* (Macmillan, 1910), p.lxxxv.
3. For example, P. Barnett identifies twenty allusions (*The Birth of Christianity: The First 20 Years,* Eerdmans, 2005, pp.128-32).

**Chapter 1 — Who's who?**
1. There are no such doubts about the ossuary of Joseph Caiaphas, the high priest who presided over the trial of Jesus, which was accidentally discovered in 1990, with those of his family, in a cave just outside Jerusalem. This is on display in the Israel museum. No one is certain, however, where the James ossuary came from.
2. Eusebius, *Historia Ecclesiastica,* II, xxiii.

**Chapter 3 — Unconventional wisdom**
1. The root meaning of *haplōs* is 'single' — hence the idea of giving with no ulterior motive, or single-minded giving. Contextually this is more likely since James goes on to speak of the double-minded man. The cognate is used in Luke 11:34 to refer to the 'single' eye.

**Chapter 6 — God is good**
1. Eta Linnemann, *Historical Criticism of the Bible,* Baker, 1990, p.18.

**Chapter 8 — Hearing aids**
1. J. Stott, *Essential Living; The Sermon on the Mount,* IVP, 1978, p.209.

**Chapter 9 — Give me that old-time religion**
1. Iain H. Murray, *Evangelicalism Divided,* Banner of Truth, 2000, p.255.

**Chapter 11 — Why favouritism is wrong**
1. J. Calvin, *Institutes of the Christian Religion,* trans. F. L. Battles, SCM Press, 1960, book II, ch. VII, para.13.

**Chapter 12 — Faith: dead or alive?**
1. The question is so phrased as to expect the answer, 'No, of course not!' Also the NIV and most modern English translations take the inclusion of the definite article before **'faith'** (literally it reads, 'Can *the* faith save him?') as referring back and specifying the unsubstantiated faith that this man claims to have. In order to bring out this distinction the NIV translates the definite article as 'such': **'Can *such* faith save him?'**(italics added). A number of other versions translate the article as 'that': 'Can *that* faith save him?'
2. G. Machen, *The New Testament,* Banner of Truth, 1976, p.239.

**Chapter 13 —Grace: 'light and easy'**
1. C. H. Spurgeon, 'The Obedience of Faith', a sermon delivered on 21 August 1890 at the Metropolitan Tabernacle.
2. D. Bonhoeffer, *The Cost of Discipleship,* SCM, 1959, p.36.
3. Peter H. Davids, *The Epistle of James, NIGTC,* Eerdmans/Paternoster, 1982, p.130.
4. For a helpful discussion of the New Perspective in particular and justification in general see Philip H. Eveson, *The Great Exchange,* Day One Publications, 1996.
5. This arises because in the English language we use two different roots to translate the one Greek root '*dik*' (*dikaios, dikaioō, dikaiosunē*): 'right' — giving a family of words, 'right' (adjective), 'to consider righteous' (verb) and 'righteousness' (noun); and 'just' — giving 'just', 'to justify' and 'justification'. This is hidden in our English translations, and readers of the Bible without access to its original Greek text will not be aware of these underlying similarities.
6. *Westminster Confession of Faith,* ch. XVI, para. V.

**Chapter 14 — Teachers of the Word**
1. J. R. W. Stott, *Between Two Worlds,* Hodder & Stoughton, 1982, p.113.

**Chapter 15 — The tongue of fire**
1. J. Blanchard, *Truth for Life,* Evangelical Press, 1986, p.198.

**Chapter 18 — The remedy for worldliness**
1. Charles Dickens, *David Copperfield,* Penguin, rev. ed., 2004, p.244.

**Chapter 22 — Waiting patiently until the coming of the Lord**
1. D. Thomas, *The Storm Breaks — Job simply explained,* Evangelical Press, 1995, p.320.

**Chapter 24 — A prayer for all seasons**
1. '*Annus mirabilis*' means 'a wonderful year'.

Sales of this book help to promote the missionary work of EP in making good Christian literature available at affordable prices in poorer countries of the world and training pastors and preachers to teach God's Word to others.